PRESIDING OVER
A DIVIDED WORLD

PRESIDING OVER
A DIVIDED WORLD
CHANGING UN ROLES, 1945–1993

ADAM ROBERTS
BENEDICT KINGSBURY

LYNNE
RIENNER
PUBLISHERS

BOULDER
LONDON

Published in the United States of America in 1994 by
Lynne Rienner Publishers, Inc.
1800 30th Street, Boulder, Colorado 80301

and in the United Kingdom by
Lynne Rienner Publishers, Inc.
3 Henrietta Street, Covent Garden, London WC2E 8LU

Library of Congress Cataloging-in-Publication Data
Roberts, Adam.
    Presiding over a divided world : changing UN roles, 1945–1993 /
Adam Roberts and Benedict Kingsbury.
      p. cm.—(International Peace Academy occasional paper
series)
    Includes bibliographical references
    ISBN 1-55587-519-X (pbk. : acid-free paper)
    1. United Nations—History. I. Kingsbury, Benedict. II. Title.
III. Series.
JX1977.R534 1994
341.23—dc20   94-4467
                                              CIP

British Cataloguing in Publication Data
A Cataloguing in Publication record for this book
is available from the British Library.

Printed and bound in the United States of America

       The paper used in this publication meets the requirements
∞ of the American National Standard for Permanence of
       Paper for Printed Library Materials Z39.48-1984.

CONTENTS

5

ACRONYMS

ECOSOC		Economic and Social Council (of the UN)
FAO		Food and Agriculture Organization
GATT		General Agreement on Tariffs and Trade
IAEA		International Atomic Energy Agency
IBRD		International Bank for Reconstruction and Development (the World Bank)
ICJ		International Court of Justice
ILO		International Labour Organisation
IMF		International Monetary Fund
NATO		North Atlantic Treaty Organization
NGO		nongovernmental organization
ONUC	*	Opération des Nations Unies au Congo (United Nations Operation in the Congo, 1960–1964)
PLO		Palestine Liberation Organization
SWAPO		South West Africa People's Organization
UK		United Kingdom of Great Britain and Northern Ireland
UN		United Nations
UNCTAD		United Nations Conference on Trade and Development
UNDP		United Nations Development Programme
UNEF	*	United Nations Emergency Force (Suez Canal, Sinai, etc.: I—1956–1967; II—1973–1979)
UNEP		United Nations Environment Programme
UNESCO		United Nations Educational, Scientific, and Cultural Organization
UNHCR		Office of the United Nations High Commissioner for Refugees
UNICEF		United Nations Children's Fund
UNITAF		Unified Task Force (US-led multistate force in Somalia, 1992–1993)
UNO		United Nations Organization
UNOSOM	*	United Nations Operation in Somalia (I—1992–1993; II—1993–present)
UNPROFOR	*	United Nations Protection Force (former Yugoslavia, 1992–)
US		United States
USSR		Union of Soviet Socialist Republics
WHO		World Health Organization

* UN peacekeeping force

1

INTRODUCTION

In the half century since its foundation in 1945, the United Nations has been a central institution in the conduct of international relations. Liberated from the particular constraints imposed by the Cold War, the UN has undertaken much more in the past few years than ever before. Yet the flush of post–Cold War enthusiasm only temporarily masked its underlying limitations.

Several fundamental problems that are now resurfacing require attention, and the UN faces a number of critical decisions about its future role and direction. Key subjects of concern include its control and management of the use of force; its difficulties in coping with problems of deeply divided societies; conflicts between sovereignty and the enforcement of international standards; problems of representation on the Security Council; slow progress on South-North issues; and the question of possible revision of the Charter.

These issues cannot be confronted effectively unless there is a core of common understanding of the nature of the UN and its place in international relations. Building such an understanding is particularly problematic because, throughout its history, the UN has been beset by conflicting and overly simple interpretations:

* The UN is a talking-shop backed by a bloated bureaucracy that achieves little of value, wastes a great deal of money, is not answerable to a democratic electorate, and will always lack the significance of governments of sovereign states.
* The UN is effective principally as a convenient instrument of avoidance, in which discussion is a cosmetic substitute for action and which states use to avoid blame for their own inaction.
* The UN is a thinly disguised servant of the interests of the

North in general and the United States in particular. This
description applies to the operation of the Security Council
and to such agencies as the International Monetary Fund
(IMF) and the International Atomic Energy Agency (IAEA).
* The UN represents a higher set of standards for the conduct
of international relations transcending the narrow interests of
states, and if allowed to function properly it offers the best
hope of eliminating the scourge of war.
* The UN is at last free of the paralysis imposed upon it by the
Cold War and finally offers the prospect of realizing the original Charter vision, or even of moving beyond that vision to a
new world system of peace and security, in which obstacles
arising from state sovereignty are eventually overcome.

This paper picks up elements of these reductionist interpretations but argues that policy must be based on a much more nuanced
evaluation. It suggests that while the UN has achieved much, it has
not, and very likely will not, overcome many of the problems that
have in the past bedeviled efforts at collective security and global
organization.

The United Nations has played important roles that individual
states or regional organizations could not themselves perform. It can
be most effective if the design and management of the UN as an institution take adequate account of the heterogeneity of the international system, the perennial character of many of the problems with
which it is confronted, and the realities and constraints of the international society within which it operates. The UN has only a limited
capacity to challenge the wills of particular states: many of its instruments for doing so—including condemnations, sanctions, and war-
crimes tribunals—are problematic. It can only act effectively where its
actions are broadly consistent with the policies of most member states
centrally involved in any particular issue.

In the confused circumstances of the post–Cold War era, the UN
faces new opportunities but also new hazards. The East-West divide
was only one of several fundamental divisions in international society.
The removal of this constraint offers scope for more effective action,
but not for the rapid realization of a utopian vision of international
organization: overreaching will result in failure and the disappointment of inflated expectations.

2

THE UNITED NATIONS AND
INTERNATIONAL SOCIETY

The international system over which the UN in some sense presides is historically unique. For the first time in human history, the world has come to consist of nominally equal sovereign states; almost all of them are members of one world organization and subscribe to a single set of principles—those of the UN Charter; and there is a functioning global organization that has the capacity to make important decisions, especially in the sphere of security—as was done in the Gulf crisis of 1990–1991. Yet despite these unique elements that distinguish the UN era from earlier times, international society remains "anarchical." In international relations usage, *anarchical* connotes neither a situation of chaos and the uncontrolled violence of a war of all against all nor the faithless "mere anarchy . . . loosed upon the world" in W. B. Yeats's *The Second Coming:* rather, the term seeks to capture the reality that there is order of a kind and a wide range of international institutions but no central dominant locus of authority and enforcement.[1] This special and complex position is well expressed by the simultaneous recognition that an international society exists, but that it is characterized in part by anarchy.[2]

The UN era has also been notable for the continuing—and in many respects burgeoning—role in international society of actors other than states.[3] The UN itself has provided a political space in which nongovernmental organizations may operate, especially in such fields as human rights and environmental protection, and it has provided forums in which all manner of nonstate groups can articulate demands and pursue their interests. More generally, some analysts have argued that a transnational civil society is beginning to emerge, constructed upon the growing density and ease of cross-border interactions and characterized by the diffusion or contagion of multiparty democracy, market liberalism, and related political and

11

social values.[4] In this view, power is shifting from increasingly enmeshed states to cross-state groupings or to international institutions; territoriality is declining as a central principle of organization; and state sovereignty is being recast to accommodate human rights, economic aspirations, and internal and external conceptions of legitimacy.[5] Perceptions of what constitutes national interest are broadening, and the normative convergence at the domestic, transnational, and international levels is progressing to the extent that these levels are beginning to merge. The European Union has been a popular model for proponents of the thesis that state sovereignty is gradually being transcended and that international civil society is being established by progressive enlargement from a liberal heartland.

International society is indeed changing, as are the issues and forms of its politics. Particular states or societies cannot easily remain outside the core institutions of economic, social, and political interaction. There are changes in the nature, forms, and uses of power, some of which result from interdependence or from the asymmetries of power that frequently accompany interdependence.[6] There are shared norms and values, which the UN both reflects and projects. Not all states work well, and the state is perhaps not held sacrosanct as the building block of international society to the extent that it was earlier in the twentieth century. Nevertheless, the state remains the principal institution for achieving domestic order, and the interstate system continues to provide the ordering framework for international society. The UN as an organization created and maintained by states is built upon an intergovernmental framework that some critics find unrealistic or unsatisfactory. Proposals for reshaping the framework, for instance by establishing a nationally elected parliamentary assembly alongside the General Assembly, may attract greater interest in the future. But for the time being the structures and activities of the UN, though in some tension with the changing circumstances and needs of international society, necessarily continue to reflect the essential role of states and the difficulties of the contemporary states system.

In the post–Cold War era the international system is beset by a bewildering multitude of problems, many of which derive from ancient and enduring features of international politics. Although the East-West divide of the Cold War period has largely disappeared, the world is still divided into separate sovereign states with differing interests, types of government, and worldviews. There are other fundamental divisions: North and South; regional animosities; differences between civilizations; and communal cleavages that in many cases cut through state lines and across frontiers, raising challenges for the existing domestic and international order.[7] Power still counts, whether in the decisionmaking processes of the UN or in the wider and messier realities beyond. The specter of war, both civil and international, has not been banished. Many urgent crises that crowd the UN's agenda today derive from these divisions.

Global international organizations that proclaim their goal to be the radical restructuring of the unsatisfactory condition of international relations inevitably attract high hopes—and subsequent disappointment.[8] This pattern has been true of the various communist internationals since the First International was founded in 1864, and of the League of Nations, founded in 1919–1920. The UN has had its fair share of such disappointed hopes and will again. Yet it has achieved a utility, an institutional durability, and even a degree of permanence that eluded its predecessors.

In the immediate aftermath of the Cold War, an attractively teleological view of the UN's place in the international order gained some currency. Proponents of this view argued that in 1945 the UN was intended to be an essentially supranational body. For over four decades, during which the world had been divided between East and West, it was unable to act effectively; indeed, in matters relating to war and peace it had been almost completely powerless because of the frequent threat or use of the veto in the Security Council. Then, with the end of the Cold War in the late 1980s, it was at last in a position to act more or less as its founders had supposedly intended, taking a decisive role in many crises, most notably in the Gulf in 1991. It now had an opportunity to advance, if not to world government, then at least toward a centrally regulated and well-ordered international system. Elements of such a view were evident in Secretary-General Boutros Boutros-Ghali's June 1992 report, *An Agenda for Peace*,[9] and in some of the subsequent debate on the issues it raised.[10]

This view was always open to challenge. First, it implied that the design of the UN Charter involved a sharper departure from the structure of interstate power politics than was in fact the case. Second, the UN's performance in the long decades of the Cold War was much more impressive than the picture of a stymied organization suggests. During the years of East-West hostility the UN became the world's first truly universal organization of states; helped to develop international standards on a wide range of matters, including human rights; and built up peacekeeping and diplomatic services that proved useful in addressing several conflicts. Third, since the end of the Cold War the UN has faced problems of a kind that have withstood the best efforts of the international community since time immemorial and can be expected to do so again.

Many of the divisions within and between states have become more serious in the UN era than before—not least because the UN, somewhat paradoxically, has presided over a new phase in the triumphant advance of the idea of the "sovereign state." In the wake of European decolonization and the collapse of the Soviet Union, the total number of such states has more than tripled. Many conflicts of our time have their origins in partitions and disputes following upon the end of empires and the attendant uncertainties about the legitimacy of new postcolonial states, regimes, institutions, and frontiers. Such problems have been especially marked following the disintegration of the USSR and Yugoslavia: indeed, the newly emerging regimes and frontiers were called into question more quickly there than in most former European colonies. The world is, and is likely to remain, divided into separate sovereign states that have a capacity for making war, many of which are conscious of their internal fragility and external vulnerability. Processes of integration and disintegration, cooperation and competition, liberation and domination, understanding and incomprehension, which have always characterized the system of states, will continue even if in new forms.

3

A SHORT DESCRIPTION OF
THE UNITED NATIONS SYSTEM

The origins of the term *United Nations* are to be found in the events surrounding the Washington Declaration of 1 January 1942, in which twenty-six Allied countries, which came to be called the United Nations, pledged themselves to employ their full resources against Germany, Italy, and Japan; and the Moscow Four-Nation Declaration of 30 October 1943, which frequently called the Allies "the United Nations." (These declarations are mentioned in Articles 3 and 106 of the UN Charter.)[11] The term *United Nations* thus emerged in an atmosphere of wartime hyperbole; and it was partly to distinguish itself from the wartime alliance out of which it had grown that, in its early years, the UN was very widely known as the United Nations *Organization* (UNO). This form is now used only occasionally for the limited purpose of distinguishing the UN proper (often just called "the Organization") from the specialized agencies. Not only has the wartime alliance receded into the distant past, but when it is remembered, its members are usually called "the Allies." The term *the United Nations* has long since been effectively appropriated by the international organization created in 1945.[12]

The first blueprints for the UN were drafted by the United States, the United Kingdom, the USSR, and their allies during World War II, reflecting their conceptions of the postwar international order. The Charter was finally adopted by the representatives of fifty states meeting in San Francisco in June 1945. Although the nature and work of the UN has evolved considerably, the Charter has remained virtually unchanged. The UN was formally established on 24 October 1945, when its basic constitutive instrument, the UN Charter, entered into force.

In the years since 1945 the number of member states of the UN has steadily increased, due mainly to the effects of successive waves of decolonization and disintegration of states. In 1945 the UN had fifty-one original members; by the end of 1960 it had one hundred members; by the end of 1984, 159; and by March 1994, 184. Throughout its history, the UN has had as members the great majority of existing states. Despite trends toward regional integration, there have only been occasional enduring cases of UN member states unifying to form a single larger state: Tanzania (1964), Yemen (1990), and Germany (1990).

The most conspicuous case of nonmembership was the People's Republic of China from its establishment in 1949 until 1971, during which period China was represented by the regime in Taiwan. Since 1971 the UN's claims to near-universalism have had real substance because its members include virtually all the states of the contemporary world. Nonmembers of the UN include Switzerland (which has never applied for UN membership), a number of microstates, and dependent or non-self-governing territories. Many of these nonmembers are nevertheless involved in various aspects of the UN system, and some are members of specialized agencies. Other entities that are not members of the UN include Taiwan (which does not claim to be a state separate from China and was expelled from China's seat in the UN in 1971), Northern Cyprus (which is not regarded as a state except by itself and Turkey), and Western Sahara and Palestine (which do not at present have effective governmental control of their respective territories but have received a degree of recognition by significant parts of the international community).

No member state has ever left the UN. However, during 1950 the USSR refused to participate in the Security Council and other UN organs in protest against the UN's refusal to accept the government of the People's Republic of China as representative of China, and in 1965–1966 Indonesia temporarily withdrew from the UN. In some cases the credentials of particular authorities as representatives of their state have not been accepted; and the Federal Republic of Yugoslavia (Serbia and Montenegro) was advised in 1992 by the Security Council and by the General Assembly that it could not continue the membership of the former Socialist Federal Republic of Yugoslavia, although it was able to continue participation in some UN bodies.

SIX PRINCIPAL ORGANS

Six "principal organs" of the UN were established by the Charter: the General Assembly, the Security Council, the Secretariat, the International Court of Justice (ICJ), the Trusteeship Council, and the Economic and Social Council (ECOSOC).

General Assembly

The General Assembly as the plenary body controls much of the work of the UN . It meets in regular session for approximately the last quarter of every year (with sessions spilling over well into the new year) and occasionally holds special or emergency sessions to consider specific issues. The General Assembly approves the budget, sets priorities, calls international conferences, superintends the operations of the Secretariat and of numerous committees and subsidiary organs, and debates and adopts resolutions on diverse issues. It played a major role in promoting the decolonization process and has also become involved in human rights supervision and election monitoring in independent countries. The many subsidiary bodies created by the General Assembly include the United Nations Children's Fund (UNICEF), the Office of the United Nations High Commissioner for Refugees (UNHCR), the United Nations Conference on Trade and Development (UNCTAD), the United Nations Development Programme (UNDP), and the United Nations Environment Programme (UNEP). Much of the work of the General Assembly is done in permanent or ad hoc committees responsible for particular fields of UN activity or deliberation. The General Assembly's agenda also includes many areas of activity in which states prefer rhetoric to real action.[13]

On a few occasions, the General Assembly rather than the Security Council has initiated peacekeeping operations: the General Assembly created the UN Emergency Force (UNEF) in the aftermath of the Suez crisis in 1956 when the Security Council was prevented by British and French vetoes from acting; it also established the UN Temporary Executive Authority in West New Guinea (West Irian) in 1962, presumably because the operation was undertaken within the framework of decolonization. In addition, it issued recommendations concerning UN forces in Korea (1950–1953) and the Congo (1960–1964) when the Security Council was blocked by veto from acting. However, control of peacekeeping has now returned firmly to the Security Council.

Security Council

The fifteen-member Security Council is dominated by its five Permanent Members (China, France, Russia, the UK, and the United States), each of which has the power to veto any draft resolution on substantive matters. The ten nonpermanent members (six until a Charter amendment came into force in 1965) are elected for two-year periods by the General Assembly. The Security Council has primary responsibility for the maintenance of international peace and security and, unlike the General Assembly, is able to make decisions that are supposed to be binding on all members of the UN . It meets almost continuously throughout the year, mainly to consider armed conflicts and other situations or disputes where international peace and security are threatened. It is empowered to order mandatory sanctions, call for cease-fires, and even to authorize military action on behalf of the UN .

The Security Council has also had a central role in the development of the institution of UN peacekeeping operations, which are not mentioned at all in the Charter. The blue berets or helmets worn by members of national military units working in the service of the UN have become a well-known symbol. UN peacekeeping operations, ranging from small observer units to larger forces for purposes of interposition, policing, and humanitarian assistance, have been established by the Security Council in numerous countries.

The Security Council has played an important role in easing or containing numerous crises, and it provides a high-level forum for diplomatic contact and negotiation. The Security Council also has a role, with the General Assembly, in the admission of new members to the UN, the appointment of the Secretary-General, and the election of judges to the ICJ.

The Charter provision that the Council must operate on the basis of unanimity among its Permanent Members was not the product of impractical idealism: the memoirs of some of those who helped frame the Charter confirm that they knew what they were doing in this as in many other respects.[14] The provision, which has been interpreted in practice to mean that any one of the Permanent Members has to vote against a resolution in order to veto it, reflects a highly realistic belief that UN action will not be possible if one of the great powers seriously dissents.

Both the actual use of the veto, and the constant possibility of its use, have been central features of the functioning of the Security Council throughout the UN's history. In the period from 1945 to the end of 1993 a total of 195 resolutions were vetoed, sometimes by more than one of the Permanent Members. Table 3.1 shows vetoes cast between 1946 and 1993.[15]

These figures reflect the fact that a Permanent Member of the Security Council can avoid direct use of the veto power if it is sure that the proposal in question will not in any event obtain the votes of

Table 3.1   Vetoes in the Security Council, 1945–1993

Year	China	France	UK	USA	USSR/ Russia	Total
1946–1955	1	2	0	0	75	78
1956–1965	0	2	3	0	26	31
1966–1975	2	2	8	12	7	31
1976–1985	0	9	11	34	6	60
1986–1993	0	3	8	23	1	35
Total	3	18	30	69	115	235

the requisite qualified majority. The Western states, in particular, were frequently able to use this tactic in the early years of the UN, while the Soviet Union used it in the 1970s and 1980s. To some extent the use of the veto has reflected diplomatic isolation of the vetoing state(s) on the particular issue, and forcing such resolutions to a vote has been a diplomatic strategy to demonstrate the isolation of the state using the veto.

Because of the veto, the Security Council could contribute little to the amelioration of many armed conflicts in which its Permanent Members were directly involved—for example, Suez (1956), Hungary (1956), Vietnam (1946–1975), the Sino-Vietnamese war (1979), and Afghanistan (1979–1988). Since the late 1980s the Security Council has had a more central role in international security, discussed in Chapter 8 of this paper. If threat or use of the veto were to again become a persistent obstacle to Security Council action, the contentious question of using the 1950 Uniting For Peace resolution might well resurface. In that resolution the General Assembly asserted the power to make recommendations on matters concerning international peace and security where the Security Council was prevented by the veto from acting. It is unlikely that states using the veto will be any more willing than previously to accept the General Assembly recommending action in such circumstances.

The period from 31 May 1990 (when the United States vetoed a resolution on the Israeli-occupied territories) to 11 May 1993 (when Russia vetoed a resolution on the financing of the peacekeeping force in Cyprus) was notable as the longest without use of the veto in the history of the UN . This was the only veto cast in 1993, but the possibility of use of the veto has continued to influence debates, proposals, and decisions on many issues, including policy regarding Bosnia-Herzegovina.

The rise in the numbers of resolutions adopted each year by the Security Council parallels the increase in its activity since 1989. Until 1989 the average had been about 15 resolutions per annum. The figures for the four calendar years 1990 to 1993 were 37, 42, 74, and 93.

Secretariat

The UN Secretariat, which is headed by the Secretary-General, comprises some fourteen thousand people at UN headquarters in New York and at other UN offices (the largest of which is Geneva). The UN Charter requires that merit is to be the paramount consideration in employment, but the UN has not always been able to adhere unswervingly to this principle. While the nature and quality of the UN's work depends greatly on the comparatively "faceless" Secretariat, the Secretary-General is also a significant figure in international diplomacy as are some of his special representatives and key staff.

The role of the Secretary-General has developed significantly since 1945. The Secretary-General has taken on—or has had forced upon him—a wide range of functions: fact-finding; mediating in disputes between states; and responding to rapidly moving crises in which other UN bodies, because of disagreement among members or the sheer pace of events, have only limited possibilities of doing anything. In particular, the Secretary-General has had a key role in proposing the establishment and composition of peacekeeping forces and in supervising their deployment and operations.

International Court of Justice

The International Court of Justice is the successor to the Permanent Court of International Justice, which was established at The Hague in 1922. The ICJ's Statute was adopted in 1945 at the same time as the UN Charter, and all UN member states are parties, as are certain other states. The ICJ is empowered to issue binding decisions in cases between states that have in some way consented to its jurisdiction. It also provides advisory opinions when requested to do so by competent international organizations. In the period from its foundation in 1946 to 31 December 1992 forty-one contentious cases reached final disposition, and twenty-one advisory opinions were delivered.

Trusteeship Council

The Trusteeship Council supervised the transition of UN Trust Territories to self-government or independence under the

International Trusteeship Systems. This objective has been achieved for all eleven UN Trust Territories except Palau (a small part of the Trust Territory of the Pacific Islands), so the council does not at present have an active role.

Although the activities of the Trusteeship Council have been limited to UN Trust Territories, the principles of the trusteeship system had a significant impact on decolonization of other non-self-governing territories. Nevertheless, within the UN the main pressure for general decolonization in the 1960s and 1970s came from other quarters: from the Special Committee on Decolonization, dominated by Third World states; and from the General Assembly's Fourth Committee.

Economic and Social Council

The Economic and Social Council comprises fifty-four states (eighteen in the UN Charter, progressively increased in 1965 and 1973). They are elected by the General Assembly. Many nongovernmental organizations (NGOs) also participate in its proceedings on a consultative basis. It supervises the work of numerous commissions, committees, and expert bodies in the economic and social fields; and endeavors, so far with only limited success, to coordinate the efforts of the many UN specialized agencies in this area.

OTHER BODIES

The UN system extends beyond the six organs created by the Charter and the various subsidiary bodies established subsequently by the UN to include a host of specialized agencies with their own separate constitutions, memberships, and budgets. These agencies constitute a distinct part of the UN system. In the words of Article 57 of the Charter, they are "established by intergovernmental agreement" and have "wide international responsibilities, as defined in their basic instruments, in economic, social, cultural, educational, health, and related fields." There are sixteen such specialized agencies associated with the UN: apart from the financial agencies—the main ones being the IMF and the World Bank (IBRD)—the "big four" are the International Labour Organization (ILO); the Food and Agriculture Organization (FAO); the United Nations Educational, Scientific and Cultural Organization (UNESCO); and the World Health Organization (WHO).[16] Other intergovernmental organizations closely associated with the UN include the General Agreement on Tariffs and Trade (GATT), which may eventually be subsumed into a proposed World

Trade Organization as a result of agreement, reached in the Uruguayan Round negotiations in 1993–1994, and the IAEA.

BUDGET

In 1992 the budget for the UN and its affiliated programs (excluding the specialized agencies) was over US$5.2 billion. There are three major modes of financing from member states: compulsory assessed contributions to the regular UN budget ($1.2 billion in 1992), compulsory assessed contributions toward peacekeeping operations ($1.3 billion in 1992), and voluntary contributions that go mainly to UN humanitarian and development programs ($2.7 billion in 1992). Thus more than half of the UN budget is financed by voluntary contributions, with most of the remainder contributed by member states in accordance with binding assessments based mainly on gross and per capita national incomes. Some costs, particularly some of those for peacekeeping, are absorbed directly by member states. The maximum share of assessments for the regular budget is 25 percent (paid by the United States), and the minimum is 0.01 percent (paid by numerous developing and ministates). For peacekeeping, greater contributions are levied on the permanent five: the United States is assessed at 30.8 percent, and the minimum is 0.001 percent. The UN has been in financial difficulties arising from nonpayment of assessed contributions since the early 1960s, and the deficit increased sharply in the 1980s. At the end of 1992 member states were $500 million in arrears to the regular budget and had accumulated $765 million in past and current peacekeeping arrears. The amounts owed for peacekeeping increased further in 1993. Despite attempts to improve this situation, reserves are inadequate, and the UN continues to face serious cash-flow problems, making management and planning unnecessarily difficult.[17]

4

PROBLEMS OF EVALUATING
THE UNITED NATIONS

International organizations present peculiarly difficult problems of evaluation. In view of the fundamental importance of many international issues and the limited powers of states to deal satisfactorily with them, the needs that could potentially be filled by an international organization of general competence such as the UN are almost limitless. Different states and groups see these needs differently: they have formed their own expectations and evaluate the UN by different yardsticks.

The UN is too often evaluated by standards unrelated to its actual capacities. Some have judged it against the standard of a prototype world government, or at least as a means of eliminating completely the international plague of war.[18] Such expectations were built up at the time of the UN's foundation. Even now, many see the organization in idealistic terms (sometimes reflecting the language of the Charter) as standing on a higher moral plane than the states of which it is composed, especially because of its advocacy of such principles as human rights, nonuse of force, and disarmament. Others have used the nonfulfillment of these highly idealistic expectations as a starting point for bitter criticism: the UN is all talk and no action; it is an arena in which governments hypocritically proclaim one set of values while themselves practicing another; it is a vehicle for the pursuit of power politics in disguise, not for their replacement. In the late 1970s and early 1980s these critical views became more prevalent and more influential, especially in that country where idealism about the UN had once been particularly strong—the United States.[19] Such views, idealistic or dismissive, evaluated the UN in simple terms, assumed that the UN must be judged by the aspirational standards set for it in the Charter, and made few distinctions among the UN's numerous different roles.[20]

A general intergovernmental organization, be it regional or global, cannot be evaluated in quite the same terms as governments:[21] its decisionmaking and implementation powers are limited, it lacks the boundaries that define and distinguish a territorial entity, and it is always operating concurrently with governments and other entities that it does not control. Such results as are achieved are often difficult to attribute to any single body.

One long-established method of assessing the UN consists of compiling "balance sheets" of achievements. Fixation with such assessments, to which the UN has been subject to an extent almost unparalleled in any political system, seems as immutable as the Charter.[22] In fact the UN's achievements cannot be neatly entered into profit and loss columns: the attempt to do so involves crude reductionism and a misguided search for single attributions, causes, and characterizations. The difficulty of agreeing on substantive standards for judging the UN's effectiveness has heightened the tendency to focus on comforting quantitative measures such as value for money. Problems of waste, inefficiency, and corruption, important as they are, have been the subject of such magnified scrutiny as to divert attention from more fundamental evaluations of the organization.

It is not easy to evaluate the performance of the UN separately from that of the member states. The UN is, as former US Secretary of State Dean Rusk observed, a political institution whose members "are pursuing their national interests as they see them."[23] It was created by governments, and it can do little without the assent of at least the majority of them. This view is a necessary antidote to the widespread misapprehensions that the UN is in the process of superseding the states system and that the UN can and ought to take strong action on its own initiative irrespective of the views of its member states. But the UN cannot be adequately understood as simply the sum of its parts. Like all institutions, whatever their origins and power base, it has developed a life and an ethos of its own. The UN framework influences states' perceptions of their interests, the ordering of their priorities and preferences, and the possibilities they see of best advancing their interests.[24] The UN has also come to embody a limited sense of a collective interest, distinct in specific cases from the particular interests of individual states. In these respects the UN has specific functions or roles against which its performance may be evaluated, even though responsibility for the quality of this performance may lie largely with member states, as well as with individual functionaries or with features of institutional design.

A practical problem of evaluation is that the formidable quantities of documentation produced by the UN, including records of debates and reports on a wide range of topics both internal and external, in some cases shed surprisingly little light on factors influencing decisions or on the wider context in which they are made. Official records often give limited information, for example, about personal considerations, informal discussions that frequently precede formal meetings, and underlying reasons why a particular actor took a particular line. Strategic and tactical considerations, trade-offs, compromises, misunderstandings, chance occurrences, and personal agendas are seldom officially documented, and it can be especially difficult to ascertain from the documents why little or no action was taken on a particular issue.[25]

5

VARIOUS ROLES OF THE UNITED NATIONS

A general international organization has many different roles at any given time, even in respect of the same conflict or issue area; its roles can change from one period to the next and can even vary significantly from those set forth in its original constitutive instrument.

The League of Nations (established in 1920 and only formally wound up in April 1946) is generally evaluated on the basis of its primary role "to achieve international peace and security" and to avoid war.[26] In this matter it conspicuously failed. Yet the League did have some useful functions apart from the unintended one of providing an object lesson in how *not* to prevent war. The League and its associated bodies were effective in some specialized areas such as labor and health. Despite the League's many shortcomings, whether the narrowness of its membership or the inadequacies of its arrangements for keeping peace, its failure taught some important lessons. This experience helps to explain why the UN Charter provided a better framework for such an organization than the League Covenant, both in its general statements of principles and in the procedures it laid down for reaching and implementing decisions in the field of international security.

When the United Nations was established in the immediate aftermath of World War II, it was viewed, like the League of Nations, as being concerned above all with the maintenance of international peace. The UN Charter provides for a stronger system of decision-making and action to maintain or restore international peace and security than did the League Covenant. The Charter also makes greater allowance for the continued separate roles of states in international security matters, not least through its acceptance of the great-power veto, and of individual and collective self-defense even outside a UN framework. During the years of East-West rivalry its role in international peace and security sometimes seemed marginal. In the security field, although some major developments took place wholly or partly within a UN framework, many others did not. For example, many fundamental issues between the United States and the USSR, and also between countries of Eastern and Western Europe, were addressed outside UN institutions. The same is true of most security issues involving the People's Republic of China and of many elements of the Arab-Israeli conflict. In such cases, more private bilateral or multilateral frameworks were preferred because unwelcome states could be excluded and there was less pressure to follow some established UN principles and practices. However, the UN did maintain an effective involvement in many security issues, including regional conflicts in southern Africa and the Indian subcontinent. UN involvement in regional security issues has increased dramatically since the late 1980s. Yet even in this period of heightened activity, the UN remains only part of the wider international framework for addressing security concerns.

Against this background, it is not surprising that many came to see the UN's contribution as being less in the field of peace among the major powers than in other areas: defusing certain regional conflicts; advocating self-determination; assisting decolonization; codifying international law; protecting human rights; and providing a possible framework for social and economic improvement or even for redistribution of wealth on a global scale.

6

DISJUNCTIONS BETWEEN
MYTH AND REALITY

Any serious assessment of the UN's successes and failures cannot neglect the importance of myth, symbol, and drama. Nor can it neglect the contrast between the high principles espoused at the UN and the more mundane realities and controversies that have characterized much of its history.

There is a complex relation between the UN's attempts to fulfill the terms of its innumerable express mandates and its more abstract role as a symbol of both the constraints and the possibilities of international society. The UN should be judged not just by what it does in particular fields of activity, or in particular crises, but also by the way in which, through its very existence, through the influence of its Charter, through the questions it addresses, and through its diplomatic rituals, it proclaims certain values and sets the terms of international debates.

Although the UN proclaims high principles, it also reflects the faults and frailties both of individuals and of states. Although it is an institution for making decisions, it is also one for postponing them. It has a far clearer decisionmaking machinery than most international organizations, but it has also seen much putting up of proposals in the Security Council in order to have them defeated. It is an institution for punishing transgressing states, but it is also one for finding face-saving solutions. Actions and statements at, and by, the UN should not always be taken at face value.

ELEMENTS OF MYTH IN THE TERM *UNITED NATIONS*

The very term *United Nations* is a misnomer with strong elements of myth about it and has been so ever since the foundation of the UN in

28

1945. One potentially misleading element in the term is the implied claim that there is unity both within and among states. Although the very existence of the UN attests to a general unity in acceptance of an international society with certain agreed institutions, it is division, not unity, that has been the more conspicuous feature of the world since 1945, as indeed it was before that date.[27]

A related misleading element in the term *United Nations* has to do with the word *nation*. Indeed, *Divided States* might be a brutally accurate if uninspiring characterization. There is a dimension of political mythology in the "nations" part of the title "United Nations." If the term *nation,* properly used, refers to a people holding in common such attributes as ethnicity, history, culture, religion, language, and a common perception of who their enemies are, then there are few "nations" among the member states of the United Nations. Many of these states are engaged in the difficult business of "nation building" and may over time generate a sense of nationhood. Meanwhile there will continue to be deep divisions within states as well as among them—divisions of region, race, nationality, tribe, religion, and class. Nations and states are far from coterminous: witness the phenomena of divided nations, multinational states, and states with irredentist claims. Indeed, many major wars of this century, including the two world wars, originated partly in problems arising from the crucial disjunction between nation and state.[28] Yet the use of the term *nation* as supposedly synonymous with *state* or *country* is deeply ingrained in contemporary idiom, not just in the title of the UN itself but in the very word *international.* At all events, the use of such terms as *nations* and *United Nations* should not cloud judgment by conveying an excessively simple image of those complex entities, sovereign states.

UN AS THEATER

Since the adoption of the Charter in the San Francisco Opera House on 25 June 1945, the UN has been a theater for standard-setting and myth-making—for appealing to higher standards than those that commonly prevail in international relations and for holding out the promise of a better-ordered world. In *The United Nations: Sacred Drama,* which remains one of the most challenging books on the subject, Conor Cruise O'Brien suggested that the function of the UN was to act—not in the sense of taking executive action, but rather in the sense of acting in a theater. He suggested that the Charter, and much UN activity, reflected the feeling that the thing feared may be averted, and the thing hoped for be won, by the solemn and collective use of appropriate words. This prayer still converges on the United Nations—as on a holy place—at times when, as in the Cuban missile crisis in 1962, or the Middle Eastern crisis of the summer of 1967, the scourge of war seems once more to be about to descend. It is the prayer that makes the drama sacred.[29]

O'Brien saw the UN's espousal of certain ideas and principles— peace, decolonization, and multiracialism among them—as its most important contribution to international life. He conceded, however, that the UN drama swings from tragedy to farce and back again, alien to neither bathos nor buffoonery.

UNEDIFYING CONTROVERSIES

The UN has always been beset by some controversy, not all of an edifying kind. The first two Secretaries-General both ended their service on almost intolerably bad terms with the Soviet Union.[30] From 1986 on, there were accusations that Kurt Waldheim, Secretary-General from 1972 to 1981, had concealed vital facts about his past role with German occupation forces in Greece and Yugoslavia during World War II and might even have had some involvement in war crimes,[31] but there was no clear evidence that any of the decisionmakers involved in Waldheim's elections had known anything of this past at the time. McCarthyism and accusations of espionage had cast a shadow over the Secretariat by 1950,[32] and accusations of espionage against members of the UN staff have recurred periodically. The UN's perennial financial crisis began in the 1950s and early 1960s with UNEF and the Opération des Nations Unies au Congo (ONUC) and carried through into the 1980s and 1990s with the failure by many states, most notably the United States and Russia, to pay their dues to the organization. Secretaries-General have had prominent disagreements with respected senior staff members about policy questions, such as the argument that led to the departure in 1982 of Theo van Boven, the director of the UN Human Rights Centre. The specialized agencies have attracted particular controversy. The USSR and other states withdrew their cooperation from WHO in the early 1950s. The United States threatened permanent withdrawal from the ILO in the late 1970s; and the United States, UK, and Singapore withdrew from UNESCO in 1984–1985. From the 1980s onward there was sharp criticism, overwhelmingly Western, of the performance of the heads of several specialized agencies, including Amadou Mahtar

M'Bow (Director General of UNESCO 1974–1987), Edouard Saouma (Director General of FAO 1976–1993), and Hiroshi Nakajima (Director General of WHO since 1988).

7

DOCTRINES ON THE USE OF FORCE
BY STATES AND LIBERATION MOVEMENTS

The maintenance of limits on the use of force by states has been a central preoccupation of the UN throughout its existence. While the nonuse of force has remained a core principle, the UN has had to confront many difficult problems concerning its scope and also concerning its application to nonstate bodies. (The question of use of force under UN auspices is considered in Chapter 8.)

USE OF FORCE BY STATES

Articles 2(4) and 51 of the UN Charter largely restrict the right of states to use force to one circumstance: individual or collective self-defense. In the past, this restriction has usually been interpreted to mean that states have the right to use force in response to an attack on a member or other state's territory—and presumably only then. This interpretation is derived from the idea, which is perhaps too simple, that readily discernible "aggression" is the main cause of war, and that stopping aggression will stop all war. But reality has proved more complex. The UN era has seen uses of force by states in a wide range of circumstances, with Article 51 being almost routinely cited by the perpetrator in justification. These incidents have included uses of force in pursuit of territorial claims; in anticipation of a possible attack or future threat; in support of self-determination; to stop unwanted political developments within a so-called sphere of influence; by way of reprisal; to protect nationals abroad; in response to alleged terrorist acts; and to rescue victims of hijackings. In such cases, the practice of states has been modified by the words of the Charter only to a limited extent.[33]

Despite such marked divergences in the interpretation of its specific provisions, and indeed of its whole ethos, the Charter does affect the behavior of states. It has reinforced the idea that there is a strong presumption in most cases against the legitimacy of the uninvited use of force by a state outside its accepted international frontiers.[34] For example: in the years after 1973 there was no attempt by Western European countries, Japan, or the United States to seize oil resources on which they were heavily dependent after the price of oil increased phenomenally. This restraint is evidence not just of the possible adverse physical consequences that would have ensued but also of the strength of the principle of nonintervention. It is certainly hard to find an answer to the hypothetical question: In what previous era would such a situation not have resulted in intervention by some of these states?[35]

UN responses to certain invasions and occupations have led to accusations of political partiality and double standards, as in 1962 when the General Assembly failed to condemn India's invasion of Goa, and in the 1970s when it repeatedly condemned armed actions by Israel and South Africa. However, the overall tendency of UN resolutions has been to condemn most invasions and occupations, irrespective of their motives or results, except when they have occurred broadly under UN auspices; and from 1979 onward the General Assembly repeatedly demanded the withdrawal of Vietnamese forces following their December 1978 intervention in Cambodia and of Soviet forces following their December 1979 intervention in Afghanistan.[36] It later condemned the US-led invasions of Grenada in 1983 and Panama in 1989.[37] Such condemnations reflected a view widely held in the international community that force should be avoided wherever possible and that the UN should not rush to applaud even beneficent consequences of the use of force. This idea that there should be a taboo on the use of force, or at least on its first use, is thoroughly understandable in a world that is grossly overarmed.

Although the UN has tended to deplore most uses of force by states, it has not thereby avoided involvement in many of the complexities that surround the whole question of the use of force in international relations. For example, the UN may condemn what is seen by a majority as a first or illegitimate use of force, but this very condemnation may, consciously or otherwise, give some encouragement to the use of counterforce. Thus the UN's criticisms of military incursions—for example, the Israeli occupation of Arab territories since 1967, the Soviet intervention in Afghanistan in 1979, the Argentine invasion of the Falkland Islands in 1982, and the Iraqi invasion of Kuwait in 1990—have all in their way had the effect of lending some legitimacy to the subsequent armed struggles (whether by states or by liberation movements) to reverse these interventions. Furthermore, the implicit endorsement by the UN of such principles as the retrocession of colonial enclaves may have encouraged some decisions to resort to force, and there were many criticisms of UN normative declarations for allegedly giving encouragement to "terrorist" movements. Thus preoccupation with principles by no means leads inevitably to a reduction in the use of force. On the contrary, it may (whether rightly or wrongly) help justify certain uses of force. Part of the concern about developments in the UN in the 1970s and 1980s was due to a fear that this was indeed proving to be so.

USE OF FORCE BY LIBERATION MOVEMENTS

Another example of the difficulties for the UN in developing and espousing coherent principles has been in connection with an age-old question of international law and relations: In what circumstances are people entitled to engage in armed struggle against an existing state? And in what circumstances may other states assist such rebels? There are no neat general answers to these questions, which are reflections of the enduring tension between the principle of nonintervention and other fundamental priorities of states. Traditionally, states have been careful (though far from consistently so) in guarding their monopoly of the right to use force and have resisted general acceptance of any such right of nonstate groups.[38] However, states do often provide assistance to certain rebel groups in other countries, whether to destabilize an adversary regime or out of kinship or sympathy with the plight or objectives of the rebels. Such assistance, associated with many different types of political system and doctrine, and generally justified more in political than in legal terms, was a notable and often destructive characteristic of East-West relations in the Cold War period, especially in the Third World.[39] It did not disappear in the post–Cold War period: conflicts in the former Yugoslavia and former Soviet Union were among the many attestations to the enduring difficulty of bringing international rules to bear on such uses of force, especially in cases where ethnic or other special ties link combatants and their external supporters.

The UN has faced the problem of the legitimacy of support for rebel groups in several different contexts. The major attempt to address this issue, in the 1970s, was and remains controversial. Due largely to the advent of new Third World members—who were particularly critical of Israel, South Africa, Rhodesia, and continued European colonial rule in Africa and elsewhere—the UN went a long way toward recognizing the legitimacy of the use of force by a particular category of nonstate bodies, namely "national liberation movements." Thus in 1970 the General Assembly approved the "Declaration on Principles of International Law Concerning Friendly Relations and Cooperation Among States in Accordance with the Charter of the UN ," which contained the following remarkable proposition:

> Every State has the duty to refrain from any forcible action which deprives peoples . . . of their right to self-determination and freedom and independence. In their actions against, and resistance to, such forcible action in pursuit of the exercise of their right to self-determination, such peoples are entitled to seek and to receive support in accordance with the purposes and principles of the Charter.[40]

This formulation, in common with other General Assembly resolutions on the topic of self-determination, failed to establish effective criteria for determining which peoples are appropriate candidates for self-determination and which groups representing them are entitled to international support. Moreover, it was in completely unresolved conflict with another proposition asserted with equal firmness in the same declaration:

> Every State has the duty to refrain from organizing, instigating, assisting or participating in acts of civil strife or terrorist acts in another State or acquiescing in organized activities within its territory directed towards the commission of such acts, when the acts referred to in the present paragraph involve a threat or use of force.

The enunciation of apparently contradictory principles with respect to the legality of support for national liberation movements was not confined to this 1970 document. Fundamental differences of view on this matter were also manifest in the 1974 Definition of Aggression.[41]

At the diplomatic level, the UN accorded observer status in the General Assembly to the Palestine Liberation Organization in 1974[42] as well as granting various degrees of participation in UN conferences and committees to certain other national liberation movements.

The UN's general support for self-determination struggles won it respect in the postcolonial world and successfully identified the UN with the emergence to independence of many such states, including Zimbabwe and Namibia. However, aspects of its approach, particularly its support for some national liberation movements, came to be seen in the United States and elsewhere, especially from the mid-1970s to the late 1980s, as casting serious doubt on the independence and impartiality of the organization.[43] The 1975 General Assembly resolution equating Zionism with "racism and racial discrimination" was a particular focus of criticism: its revocation in 1991 was a notable symbol of a new balance between consensus and confrontation in the politics of the General Assembly.[44]

A particular problem with the resolutions actively supporting self-determination was that they said little about the question of whether any restraints should govern the methods used in self-determination struggles. Almost nothing was said about the applicability of the laws of war to combat by national liberation movements or other insurgents—a matter tackled separately, and with limited practical effect, in the 1977 Geneva Protocols I and II negotiated under the auspices of the International Committee of the Red Cross. Tactics regarded (especially in the West) as terrorism, and which were used by some national liberation movements and other insurgent groups, were addressed only slowly and in piecemeal fashion by UN bodies. A near-consensus critical of terrorism in general, though not always agreeing in particular instances, did gradually emerge.[45]

STATE-SUPPORTED TERRORISM

One aspect of terrorism posing special problems both for states and for the UN has been state support of terrorist groups and activities. The Charter system is primarily geared to dealing with organized large-scale external uses of force by states. Terrorism, in contrast, has largely been perceived as an outlaw or nonstate activity against which all states should act within their sphere of jurisdiction. Problems have arisen when states have employed terrorist methods externally through the use of more or less deniable groups; or have simply provided shelter to terrorists; or have lacked the capacity to control their activities, however unwelcome.

One response has been the use of force by states against some (but by no means all) allegedly terrorist states. In April 1986, when US aircraft bombed targets in Libya in response to terrorist attacks on US citizens overseas, it was claimed that the United States was acting in self-defense in conformity with Article 51 of the Charter.[46] Other states questioned the US interpretation of both the facts and the law. In June 1993, the United States employed similar justifications for an attack on Baghdad following alleged Iraqi government involvement in a plot to assassinate ex-President Bush in Kuwait in April. Again, the responses of other states varied. Interpretations of the right of self-defense favoring such uses of force are open to abuse, weaken the general prohibition on the use of force, and remain contentious. Another response to state terrorism has been nonforcible attempts, in some cases under UN auspices, to compel allegedly terrorist states to cease such activities or to ensure the punishment of offenders: the sanctions and other pressure imposed on Libya from 1992 onward by the Security Council with the intention of forcing Libya to surrender individuals suspected of terrorist offenses for trial abroad is a particularly prominent example.

8

COERCION AND PEACEKEEPING
UNDER UN AUSPICES

The UN Charter, principally in Chapter VII, envisaged that the UN itself would have more means of exercising pressure and coercion, and better means of decisionmaking in crises, than did the League of Nations. In order to enable the UN to deal with threats to the peace, the Security Council was seen as having responsibility for the use of sanctions of various types and for use of military forces. The overall approach of the Charter is, on one hand, to establish a system with strong elements of collective security and, on the other, to preserve the right of states to individual or collective self-defense, at least until the Security Council has taken necessary measures.

COLLECTIVE SECURITY

The term *collective security* normally refers to a system in which each state in the system accepts that the security of one is the concern of all and agrees to join in a collective response to aggression. In this sense it is distinct from systems of alliance security, in which groups of states form alliances with each other principally to oppose possible external threats.

The idea of collective security, which was aired at the negotiations that led to the 1648 Peace of Westphalia, has a history almost as long as systems of states.[47] This attractive central idea, with its many variants, has frequently proved to have fundamental flaws when tested in practice against some basic questions.[48] Among the problems are:

- defining which territories and boundaries are included within the system

- reaching agreement on whether the system covers effectively certain types of threat (e.g., acts of terrorism, environmental despoliation, genocide within a state)
- assuring participating states that the system protects them all equally
- coping with severe power imbalances within the system, especially the presence of superpowers
- defining the role of alliances
- ensuring that the system effectively deters rather than simply responds after the fact
- developing a decisionmaking procedure to reach effective and consistent determinations that a threat to or breach of the peace requiring a response has occurred and to decide what action is necessary
- agreeing on an effective system of force maintenance, command, and control
- deciding whether all participating states must maintain standing forces and provide them upon request for extraterritorial enforcement actions
- maintaining some space for established practices of neutrality in peace and war
- working out an effective system of finance, compensation, and burden-sharing
- ensuring that states do not abuse the protection of the system, or their indispensable role within it, to pursue unnecessarily confrontational policies toward other states
- determining how far collective security depends upon an effective system of disarmament and arms control, especially as regards weapons of mass destruction

After 1945, the ambitious scheme for collective security in Chapter VII of the UN Charter was not implemented.[49] The most obvious reason was the inability of the Permanent Members of the Security Council to reach agreement across the Cold War divide. Article 43 agreements, necessary to place national forces at the disposal of the UN , have never been concluded. The immediate problem was ideological mistrust, but there has also been a continuing underlying reluctance on the part of states to see their forces committed to participate in distant, controversial, and risky military operations without their express consent and command.

Such actual international security arrangements as did emerge were centered less on the UN than on bilateral and regional alliances—the latter including the Rio Treaty, North Atlantic Treaty

Organization (NATO), and the Warsaw Pact. Although Chapter VIII of the UN Charter had envisaged regional security arrangements, it had also provided for the Security Council to exercise a general supervisory role over enforcement action by such bodies: this did not materialize in practice for most of the Cold War period.

UN VARIATIONS OF THE COLLECTIVE SECURITY SCHEME

Despite the nonimplementation of fundamental aspects of the Charter scheme, the UN has developed useful methods for responding to many situations of international and internal conflict. To a large extent these methods were not provided for in the Charter, although the Charter allocation of primary responsibility to the Security Council has been respected at least since the 1960s. The UN has developed a sophisticated system of peacekeeping operations; it has adopted nonforcible sanctions under Article 41 of the Charter and made some innovative provision for their implementation and enforcement; it has authorized member states to use force in response to specific security problems; and it has been associated with a few, inevitably much debated, cases of "humanitarian intervention."

In all these matters, the Security Council has begun in a limited and incremental way to expand the scope of UN action in the post–Cold War period. The first tangible indication of the possibility of greater East-West cooperation within the UN system was the consensus of the five Permanent Members of the Security Council on Resolution 598 of 20 July 1987, demanding a cease-fire in the Iran-Iraq war (a cease-fire that was in fact achieved in 1988). The proliferation of UN activities since then, marked by increasing variety and expansion of scope, has been associated with a further blurring of the traditional lines between the established categories of UN action. Many hybrid forms are emerging within and between these categories, involving various combinations of peacekeeping, sanctions, enforcement, good offices, humanitarian assistance, political support, election monitoring, and coordinated action with states and other international organizations.

Peacekeeping Operations

Peacekeeping operations, which may take a variety of forms ranging from unarmed military observer missions to armed peacekeeping units, are essentially an ad hoc mechanism developed by the UN to assist in such purposes as containing armed conflicts and promoting cease-fires. Peacekeeping forces generally consist of separate national contingents under a unified UN -appointed command. They must normally be authorized by the Security Council but are directed on a day-to-day basis by the Secretary-General. The particular tasks of each force vary considerably and are specified in the relevant authorizing resolutions. Peacekeeping forces have generally been expected to be impartial as between the parties to a conflict. Until the early 1990s, it was a fundamental principle that they were established and deployed only with the consent of states parties to the conflict. Because they lacked enforcement power, UN peacekeeping operations were generally seen as only able to function effectively with the cooperation of the parties directly concerned. When peacekeepers were armed, they were permitted to use force only in self-defense: since 1973 the understanding of self-defense has been broadened to allow the use of force against armed persons preventing fulfillment of the mandate, although in practice peacekeeping forces have seldom used force for this more sweeping purpose.[50]

By December 1993 the UN had set up thirty-three bodies that it classified as peacekeeping operations. Thirteen of them were established between 1948 and 1978, the remaining twenty in the period since 1988. These operations have been used both in international conflicts (as between Israel and its neighbors) and in internal conflicts with international aspects (as in the Congo, Cyprus, Angola, Yugoslavia, Cambodia, Somalia, and Mozambique). During the Cold War, UN peacekeeping forces had no role in central areas of direct East-West rivalry—for example, in Hungary in 1956, in Czechoslovakia in 1968, and in Indochina from 1946 to 1991.

UN peacekeeping has in several cases failed to prevent war and unilateral intervention. In 1967, Secretary-General U Thant felt obliged to accede to the Egyptian government's request for the withdrawal of UNEF, even though it was widely understood that this action was a prologue to the war between Israel and Egypt in June of that year. In Lebanon, the presence of UN forces failed to prevent either the country's slide into anarchy and communal warfare or the Israeli invasion in 1982. In Cyprus, the UN forces that were there to keep the peace between the Greek and Turkish communities could not prevent external involvement in that communal conflict, culminating in the 1974 Turkish invasion of northern Cyprus. In Angola in 1992, UN-monitored elections were followed by a brutal renewal of the long-standing civil war.

Despite these limitations, the UN's peacekeeping activities remain one of the most significant innovations of the organization. In many matters to do with security, success is by definition almost unnoticed. The involvement of the UN has helped to isolate certain conflicts from great-power rivalry. In many cases the presence of peacekeeping forces has stabilized conflicts, but paradoxically in so doing may have reduced pressure for long-term solutions.

The traditional tasks of UN peacekeeping operations have included monitoring and supervision of cease-fires; observation of frontier lines; interposition between belligerents; and, occasionally, monitoring government and public order. Since the late 1980s such forces have been involved in monitoring and even running elections, as in Namibia, Angola, Cambodia, and Mozambique. They have assumed major roles in assuring delivery of humanitarian relief during conflicts, especially in the former Yugoslavia and in Somalia.

UN peacekeeping operations have been involved increasingly in certain essentially governmental functions, most notably in Cambodia. There have been proposals for temporary UN administration of Sarajevo as part of a Bosnian peace settlement. Yet there has been little sign of willingness on the part of the UN or its leading members to accept some kind of trusteeship role as one possible consequence of taking on responsibilities in areas where order has broken down. The historical record of various forms of mandate, trusteeship, and international administration has been mixed, but proposals for such arrangements have continued to appear in international diplomacy, and the concept may merit contemporary reconsideration.[51] In some circumstances there may be good reasons to establish a temporary externally imposed administrative system, at least when such a proposal has the active support of all parties to a dispute. The absence of an administrative role may sometimes restrict the options available to UN forces to primarily military ones.

The use of UN forces in situations of endemic intrastate conflict has increased markedly in recent years, including in Angola, Cambodia, El Salvador, Georgia, Mozambique, Rwanda, Somalia, and former Yugoslavia. In many of these cases there has not been an effective cease-fire or even any clear front lines, and the problems confronting UN forces have challenged many traditional assumptions of peacekeeping, including the principles of operating on the basis of consent, impartiality between the parties, and nonuse of force except in self-defense.

Peacekeepers in such conflicts have been under intense pressure to use force for various purposes, including delivery of humanitarian relief, punishment of attacks on UN personnel, prevention of atrocities or flagrant aggression, and compelling parties who have agreed to a peace settlement to comply with it. Such pressure to take military action has raised several problems. UN troops may have to choose between losing credibility and losing impartiality. They risk being perceived simply as one additional belligerent party and may readily become targets for retaliation.

In many situations, UN peacekeeping forces must of necessity avoid major uses of force. They may be of insufficient size, lacking in major armaments, restricted by their mandates and the views of their national governments, and lacking the popular political support to engage in major offensive operations. Yet the costs of military inaction by UN forces may also be high. As in the former Yugoslavia, UN forces may be formally defined as a protection force, yet have only limited physical power or political authority actually to protect beleaguered local communities. They may be unable to prevent or punish visible and continuing atrocities. The situation in Bosnia in 1992–1994, where the UN Protection Force (UNPROFOR) was unable to protect the inhabitants, exposed the stark problems of attempting a peacekeeping operation in a situation where there is no peace to keep. The Bosnian Muslims' perception of an ineffectual UN was compounded by the UN arms embargo on former Yugoslavia, which affected the Muslims heavily: they argued that this embargo deprived them of the right of self-defense when the UN was unable to provide any other protection.

In response to exceptionally difficult problems in former Yugoslavia, there was continuing pressure (particularly from the United States) to resort to the use of air power. Compared to involvement on the ground, air attacks involve relatively low risks to the countries and forces using this instrument. However, there was concern within the UN (including some of its commanders in the field) that the use of air power could fail to improve, and might even in some areas worsen, the situation on the ground. The uses of US helicopter gunships in Somalia in summer 1993 illustrated the shortcomings of air power as a means to make up for the limitations of peacekeeping on the ground. In Bosnia NATO's threat of air strikes did prompt a lull in fighting around Sarajevo in February 1994, but serious doubts remained about the consequences of the actual use of air strikes in an attempt to change the situation at ground level. The use of air power to enforce the Bosnian no-fly zone established by the Security Council has been less problematic, although numerous violations went unpunished until February 1994 when NATO shot down four Bosnian Serb aircraft under the authority conferred by the Security Council in March 1993.

The experience of peacekeeping operations in several countries, particularly Somalia and former Yugoslavia, has exposed the problematic relation between UN command and national commands. States supplying forces, and their commanders in the field, have remained independent decisionmakers, reluctant to defer to UN command, especially in matters relating to the safety of their troops or to the use of air power or other advanced weaponry. Where the UN lacks fire-power it has had to invoke, or in certain cases to tolerate, military actions by outside bodies: by South African forces in Namibia in April 1989, against SWAPO infiltrators; by US forces in Somalia in 1993, following attacks on UNOSOM II personnel; and by NATO air forces in former Yugoslavia in 1994. UN credibility and effectiveness may at times be impaired by national governments choosing to withdraw their forces, as in Haiti in 1993.

The UN has been compelled to confront the severe problems of peacekeeping in situations of endemic conflict but is bound to have grave difficulty in coming up with answers. The problem is not just that the UN lacks a satisfactory command system capable of making quick decisions and of effectively coordinating the many different types of forces and national contingents deployed. There is as yet lit-tle sign of the emergence of a satisfactory doctrine or practice regard-ing operations that have an essentially hybrid character, involving ele-ments of both peacekeeping and enforcement. Above all, there are limits to what international peacekeeping can achieve in the face of determined states and armed groups, especially in situations where troop-contributing states will make only a limited commitment to an operation and have difficulties in achieving and holding an interna-tional consensus on its means and objectives.

Postconflict Peace-building

One of the ways that peacekeeping forces have increasingly been mandated to go beyond the military task of imposing or maintaining cessations of hostilities has been termed *postconflict peace-building*. This term has been defined by Boutros-Ghali as "action to identify and support structures which will tend to strengthen and solidify peace in order to avoid a relapse into conflict."[52] Cases in which peacekeeping forces and other UN bodies have become involved in such action have included Cambodia (1991–1993) and El Salvador (1991–   ). Peace-building has been one response to the much-noted deficiency of some peacekeeping operations: that they merely keep the lid on a conflict and do nothing about its underlying causes. However, its limi-tations are obvious: restoring conditions of peace within and between war-torn societies is an extremely difficult task that has been a prob-lem for political leaders and diplomats over centuries. On one hand, the UN has had some successes in this field, and peace-building will be an increasingly important area of international activity. On the other hand, the UN has become involved in some intractable situations. In Somalia, events in 1993 suggested that peace enforcement or forcible peacekeeping may be inimical to peace-building in any situation short of military occupation or trusteeship. In extreme cases, *peace-building* may become a euphemism for interventionism. A normative framework for its operation, including the delicate question of its relation to self-determination and rights of political participation, has not yet been fully worked out.

Sanctions

Sanctions are an important tool available to the Security Council in responding to conflicts and threats to international peace under Chapter VII of the Charter. Unlike peacekeeping, they are envisaged in the Charter, in Article 41. Sanctions have collective security functions, that is, they can be imposed to punish acts of aggression, but they have also been initiated under other circumstances. The UN's use of sanctions, fairly rare until 1990, has had general support, but there has also been concern about their exact purposes, their effects and effectiveness.[53] General economic sanctions were applied to Rhodesia (1966–1979), Iraq following its invasion of Kuwait (1990–), and Serbia and Montenegro (1992–). An arms and air traffic embargo was imposed on Libya in March 1992, followed by more general sanctions in November 1993. There were also embargoes on the supply of arms to South Africa (1977–); former Yugoslavia (1991–), Somalia (1992–), and Liberia (1992–). Petroleum and other sanctions on Khmer Rouge–occupied areas of Cambodia were authorized in November 1992, although the Security Council did not refer to Chapter VII of the Charter. Arms and petroleum sanctions were imposed on Haiti in June and October 1993, and on the Unita rebel movement in Angola in September 1993. As many of these cases demonstrate, sanctions have symbolic functions and are often used as a form of communication of international values. They can be a means of warning an adversary of the seriousness with which a particular matter is viewed and of the prospect of more forceful action. They may also be used with the rather different purpose of assuaging domestic opinion in states taking part in the sanctions, often with the intention of avoiding military action or other unpalatable options. There can in some cases be serious questions about sanctions' compatibility with the human rights of the target state population, particularly if the instrumentalist calculation is that the people will rise up against their government if there is enough domestic suffering.

Authorization of Use of Force by States

When confronted by situations requiring the large-scale use of force, the Security Council has not itself been able, in the years since 1945, to command substantial military action in the way envisaged in Chapter VII. Its primary method for dealing with this problem has been to authorize the use of force by member states. The Security Council has authorized the use of armed forces by US-led coalitions, rather than under the command of the UN, in the cases of Korea (1950), Iraq-Kuwait (1990), and Somalia (1992).[54] UN authorization of limited use of force by states has also become a common method for enforcing sanctions, air exclusion zones, and other restrictions on particular states and activities. In the case of Bosnia-Herzegovina the Security Council in Resolution 836 of June 1993 authorized member states, acting nationally or through regional organizations or arrangements, to use air power to support UNPROFOR in and around the "safe areas" proclaimed by the UN. The Council stated that such measures were "subject to close coordination with the Secretary-General and UNPROFOR," although the precise nature and extent of the Secretary-General's power in this context has remained unresolved. The broader constitutional questions of the powers of the Secretary-General and UN force commanders in the absence of express and precise mandates have been matters of contention over four decades, and permanent solutions are not imminent.

There are advantages in an arrangement whereby forces are authorized by the Security Council but remain principally under the command of states, coalitions, or alliances. It reflects the reality that not all states feel equally involved in every enforcement action. Moreover, military action requires an extremely close relation between intelligence-gathering and operations, a smoothly functioning decisionmaking machine, and forces with some experience of working together to perform dangerous and complex tasks. These things are more likely to be achieved through existing national armed forces, alliances, and military relationships than they are within the structure of a UN command. As habits of cooperation among the armed forces of different states develop, and as the UN itself grows, the scope for action under direct UN command may increase, but it must be a slow process.

For the UN there may be risks in too direct involvement in the management of military force: when terrible mistakes occur, as they inevitably do in military operations, they reflect badly on the organization and could threaten its universal character. However, there are also risks for the UN where it is insufficiently involved: it may be seen as marginal or irrelevant to the conduct of a major operation it authorized, as happened in the Gulf in 1991 and to some extent in Somalia in 1993. In the case of Bosnia-Herzegovina in particular, Secretary-General Boutros-Ghali has struggled to assert some control or at least influence over the conduct of UN-authorized operations. For example, he sought to ensure that any NATO air strikes would be at the request of the UN, and to this end delegated to his Special Representative for the former Yugoslavia, Yasushi Akashi, authority to approve such requests.[55]

Humanitarian Intervention

In some of its involvements from 1991 onward, the Security Council collectively, and its Western Permanent Members individually, were seen by many as taking some hesitant steps toward a new doctrine and practice of humanitarian intervention—that is, military intervention in a state without the approval of its authorities, and with the purpose of preventing widespread suffering or death among the inhabitants.[56]

The UN Security Council expressly attached great importance to the delivery of humanitarian aid and to other humanitarian concerns in several crises, including those over the Kurds in northern Iraq beginning in 1991, and former Yugoslavia and Somalia beginning in 1992. In respect of Iraq, the Security Council did say in resolution 688 of 5 April 1991 (which received only ten affirmative votes) that it "insists that Iraq allow immediate access by international humanitarian organizations to all those in need of assistance in all parts of Iraq." However, such legal justification as could be furnished for the US-led Operation Provide Comfort that followed lay in a view of customary law or in a very broad interpretation of the mandate in resolution 678 of November 1990 "to restore international peace and security in the area." The operation has to be seen partly in the special context of postwar actions by victors in the territory of defeated adversaries. Further, there were elements of Iraqi consent in the subsequent presence of UN guards in northern Iraq. Regarding the UN's involvement in former Yugoslavia, there were some suggestions in the Security Council resolutions that if UNPROFOR and its humanitarian activities were obstructed, further measures not based on the consent of the parties might be taken to deliver humanitarian assistance.[57] In Somalia, there was no government to give or refuse consent, so theUN-authorized intervention by the Unified Task Force (UNITAF) in December 1992, and its continuation by the second UN operation in Somalia (UNOSOM II) in May 1993, can hardly be seen as a classic case of humanitarian intervention. In order to act under Chapter VII, as it did in each of these three cases, the Security Council's action must be premised upon the existence of a threat to international peace and security. However, once a consensus has emerged that action is warranted (whether on humanitarian or other grounds), this requirement has not proved a major obstacle.

The experience of these cases since 1991 provides further evidence that there are a number of difficulties associated with the idea of humanitarian intervention. The very label *humanitarian intervention* is an oversimplification. Military involvements may have more complex motives, purposes, and effects than the phrase implies, and their character may change markedly over time. Elements of the population of the target state frequently come to resent the impact of prolonged intervention on local decisionmaking and to oppose the presence of foreign forces.

There seems to be little prospect of the majority of states formally agreeing to any new general doctrine of humanitarian intervention. Indeed, there remains a very strong commitment among many states to the principle of nonintervention. What has occurred is a subtly developing practice in special circumstances, in which some degree of authority from the Security Council has a significant part.

PROBLEMS OF CONTROL OF UN FORCES

As UN forces get involved in more complex missions in which neat distinctions between humanitarian missions, peacekeeping, and enforcement are eroded, the adequacy of the UN's existing machinery for controlling operations is increasingly called into question. In 1992–1993, leading figures connected with UN peacekeeping activities in both Somalia and Bosnia-Herzegovina had significant disagreements with UN Headquarters in New York. The UN Special Representative for Somalia, Mohammed Sahnoun, resigned on 26 October 1992; and the former head of UN forces in Sarajevo, Major-General Lewis MacKenzie, made a forceful complaint about UN management of operations.[58] That there were problems of supply, command, and control and a need to strengthen both the staff in New York and headquarters in the field was readily acknowledged in the Secretariat: the eventual responses included the creation in 1993 of a "situation room" in UN Headquarters to keep it linked with all peacekeeping operations.[59] Nevertheless, the capacity of the UN itself to conduct certain forms of large-scale operations, especially where a stable peace does not exist, and difficult military decisions have to be taken quickly, remains limited. Moreover UN forces are not immune from ill discipline, blunders, and accusations of partisanship and neo-colonialism.[60]

Availability of Armed Forces to the UN

The increasing scope of UN activity in the post–Cold War era has raised the issue of the resuscitation of the extensive Chapter VII provisions for the Security Council itself to have armed forces on call and to make plans for their use through its Military Staff Committee. *An Agenda for Peace,* paragraph 43, advances the idea that the UN Security Council might have forces available on a permanent basis, in accord with Article 43, as one means of increasing its credibility and its power to deter. However, this report offers no serious discussion of the reasons why states have traditionally been nervous about proposals for making forces permanently available to the UN. States seem to prefer that the provision of military force for UN activities be managed in an ad hoc manner, giving them greater control over events. States still guard their power jealously, including their power to decide the exact circumstances in which their armed forces will or will not be used.

Permanent large-scale transfer of forces to the UN in advance of any crisis remains improbable. However, there has been progress on the earmarking, preparation, and training of national military units for possible UN use. This development conforms roughly with the modest proposal advanced by Boutros-Ghali in 1993 that national force structures could be broken down into standard "building blocks" of operational capability, available to the UN on a standby basis.[61]

One alternative idea—of a standing UN force comprised of professionals recruited on a voluntary basis—has been advanced by Sir Brian Urquhart.[62] Such a force would have the merit of giving the Secretary-General a capacity for a fast military response in certain crises, for example, in assisting a state threatened by external attack. However, the proposal faces problems. It is of limited relevance to certain key challenges faced by the UN . The crises in Somalia and Bosnia have cast doubt on the capabilities of even quite large professional forces to carry out difficult tasks: in these cases it is more the fact of involvement and the specific mandates of the forces that are the main issues for debate. Further, the volunteer force proposal has run up against the familiar problem that governments seem resistant to seeing the UN with an independent military capacity, and to financing it.

The Military Staff Committee

There has been extensive discussion of breathing some life into the UN Military Staff Committee, established under Article 47 of the Charter and comprising military representatives of the five Permanent Members. Although the committee has met regularly, it has been notoriously ineffective. This ineffectiveness was often seen as a consequence of the Cold War but continued into the 1990s despite improvements in relations among the Permanent Members: the Western members in particular have remained skeptical about putting enforcement, or even peacekeeping, operations under the strategic direction of such a disparate committee. There is little prospect at present of realizing the Charter vision of unified strategic direction of major military operations by the committee. In this area practice is likely to continue to diverge from the Charter. However, the committee has been used for informal exchanges, as in the 1990–1991 Gulf crisis. It could conceivably address such matters as the development of rules of engagement and the harmonization of rules of war as they affect multilateral forces, and it could even tender military advice on general issues.

THE UN'S SECURITY ROLES

Although the UN has been much more actively involved in military and other action to maintain the peace than many expected after the rapid disintegration of the World War II alliance, its principal activities have been markedly different from those foreshadowed in the Charter. Boutros-Ghali's *An Agenda for Peace* presents a vision of the UN playing a central role in international security matters; this vision includes peacekeeping but is otherwise close to the scheme of the Charter. While many of the ideas he presents—including increased peacekeeping activities and preventive deployments of forces to stop threatened invasions—have been implemented in some recent UN operations, the realities are likely to remain more difficult and complex than this vision allows. Differences of perceptions and interests among states, prominent in the Cold War period, continue to be pronounced, making united action on security issues uncertain and difficult. Peacekeeping works well only when there is a peace to keep, and in some situations the cost of trying to impose peace is too high. In civil conflicts in particular, peacekeeping and enforcement action may be close to impossible, especially in situations where communal hatreds have become deep-seated, there are no viable geographical lines separating combatants, and the types of weapons used are easily available and difficult to control.

The Charter scheme does not deal specifically with the question of breakdown of order within states and the outbreak of communal war. Nonetheless, since very early in the UN's history, states have seen the UN as a convenient repository for many such difficult problems. In some such cases, including El Salvador from 1991 onward, the UN has contributed to the achievement of political solutions. However, the complexity of these problems makes UN involvement risky in each case and repeatedly forces unsatisfactory choices about whether and how to get involved. Political dynamics often impair careful judgment about prospective involvements.

The record of actions under UN auspices, while too significant to deserve the pejorative label *selective security*, has been too patchy to constitute a reliable system of collective security. In a large number of major cases the UN has not acted at all; indeed, in some it has not been asked to act even by the victim of apparent aggression. When it has acted, many of the means employed have been problematic, both because of the difficulty of the issues and because of the reluctance of states to commit themselves deeply or take great risks. Despite important exceptions, there has been a tendency to prefer methods of remote control (economic sanctions, air exclusion zones, arms embargoes, attempts to broker cease-fires, aerial bombardment) or limited involvement with the consent of the parties (peacekeeping, observer, and humanitarian activities). A further problem associated with UN-controlled operations is the rigidity of their mandates and rules of engagement. The fact that the mission of UN forces has to be the subject of advance international agreement can seriously reduce their flexibility in fast-changing situations, leading to criticism from both within and outside.

9

POSSIBLE CHANGES IN THE COMPOSITION AND POWERS OF THE SECURITY COUNCIL

The need to reform or strengthen the UN has been argued with passion since its inception.[63] Many proposals for change have focused on the Security Council. The UN Charter provisions regarding its composition, procedures, and powers have long been the subject of criticism. It is especially natural that these matters should be debated when, as in the post–Cold War era, the Security Council actually wields considerable power. However, the problem of Security Council membership and powers is tangled. A key difficulty is identifying and agreeing on reforms that would not undermine, or might even enhance, the Council's capacity to make effective decisions.

Criticism of the composition of the Security Council involves several elements: doubt about preserving unaltered, half a century later, the special position of the countries that were allies in World War II; concern that three of those powers—France, the UK, and the United States—make most of the running in the Security Council; irritation, especially on the part of Germany and Japan, about "taxation without representation"; frustration that the views of the nonpermanent members of the Security Council, and indeed of the great majority of the General Assembly, count for little; and concern that in half a century the Security Council has been enlarged only modestly, from eleven to fifteen members, while the General Assembly has more than tripled in size. These criticisms could become much more serious if perceptions of the Security Council having pursued unacceptable or ill-advised policies on central issues mount appreciably.

It is natural that over time, as circumstances change, there should be pressures for reform of the arrangements regarding the composition of the main decisionmaking body of an international organization. Whether such reforms will lead to a better decisionmaking process is, inevitably, uncertain. One unpromising precedent is that between 1922 and 1936 the number of nonpermanent members of the League of Nations Council was successively increased from four to eleven—a reform that was of marginal relevance to the larger question of the League's capacity to act effectively.

CHARTER REVISION

Change of the UN Security Council's composition is by no means impossible: in 1965, through amendment to Article 23 of the Charter, the number of nonpermanent members was increased from six to ten. Today there are various widely canvassed proposals for further expansion. Japan and Germany have often been named as possible Permanent Members of the Security Council, especially in US statements.[64] In June 1993, pursuant to General Assembly Resolution 47/62 of 11 December 1992, the United States informed the Secretary-General that it "supports permanent membership for Japan and Germany," that it was "also prepared to consider carefully how the Council might be further expanded to include a modest number of additional seats," and that other means of involving nonmembers of the Council should be explored.[65] However, there is bound to be resistance to any proposal that would give two conspicuously Northern states the same status as the five, while leaving out Brazil, Egypt, India, Indonesia, Nigeria, and others. Any proposed increase in the total number of Permanent Members with the veto would also attract opposition. Thus many influential proposals for Charter amendment involve either a new category of Permanent Member without veto or, perhaps most likely of any proposed changes, an expansion of the number of nonpermanent members, possibly with some relaxation in the requirement of a two-year standdown after every two years of membership.

The veto system privileges a group of five states in a way that is bound to provoke contention, and it is widely perceived as having held the UN back from fulfilling its functions in the Cold War years. Yet the veto has merits as well as faults: it helped to get and keep the major powers within a UN framework when they would otherwise have either not joined it in the first place or else deserted it; it may have saved the UN from damaging conflicts with its major members and from involvement in divisive or impossible missions; it has contributed to a sense of responsibility and a habit of careful consultation among the permanent five; and it reduces the risk of acute discrepancies between power politics and the law of the Charter. In short, the veto can be viewed as one of several factors that have made for the superiority of the UN's decisionmaking procedures over those of its predecessor, the League of Nations, and over many regional organizations.

Modification or abandonment of the veto would be problematic. The procedures governing Charter amendment make any change affecting this power particularly difficult, as the consent of the countries concerned would be required. Article 108 stipulates that all Charter amendments must be adopted by two-thirds of the members of the General Assembly and be ratified, in accord with their respective constitutional processes, by two-thirds of the members of the UN, including all Permanent Members of the Security Council. There seems to be very little prospect of China, Russia, or the United States agreeing to weaken its veto power.

Membership in the permanent five entails heavy costs as well as privilege. In problematic UN undertakings, the Permanent Members risk direct association with failure. Membership also involves assuming a larger share of costs of peacekeeping forces[66] and in some cases pressure to follow up votes in the Security Council with the commitment of forces in crisis-torn areas. That power has its rewards is indicated by the tenacity with which Britain and France hang on to their position as members of the permanent five. Yet the overextension of Britain's and France's capabilities, so familiar in the nineteenth century, may be reemerging in UN colors.

Meanwhile, other states have vetoes of a kind on enforcement actions. First, there is the so-called sixth veto on the Security Council—the capacity of Security Council members to defeat a resolution by denying it the nine affirmative votes needed to pass. Second, despite the words of the Charter, states do not have to take part in enforcement or peacekeeping operations if they do not so wish. In the matter of use of their forces, they are not mere pawns of the UN .

In the history of the United Nations, much has been achieved by changes in practice rather than Charter revision. For example, Russia's succession to the USSR's Security Council seat was handled by such means in December 1991–January 1992, and Article 23 was not amended. Further changes in Security Council practice could include strengthening existing arrangements so that the selection of nonpermanent members more closely reflects contributions to the UN's work as well as equitable geographical distribution; and developing more regular Security Council consultation with major states and interested parties. Such changes, though hard to implement when UN decisionmaking procedures are so overloaded, might go at least some way toward meeting the strong concerns of certain states about being left out of decisions that affect them vitally.[67]

CONTROLS ON THE SECURITY COUNCIL

Just as the power of national governments needs to be subject to both internal and external constraints, so the UN , even the Security Council, is far from infallible and requires a system of controls. The UN faces the familiar constitutional problem of maintaining and enhancing the effectiveness of the Security Council while simultaneously ensuring that the Council is subject to adequate controls. The Council is constrained by the general prudence of member states and the factual limitations of what is actually possible. Other long-established controls—many of which have also limited the Council's effectiveness—include the composition and voting rules of the Council, its inability to commit forces without the express consent of the troop-contributing states, limitations on the effective enforcement of sanctions, and budgetary constraints through the General Assembly. Difficulties remain in devising controls on contentious actions by the Security Council in several situations: where the Council takes an exceptionally wide view of what constitutes a threat to or breach of the peace, thus investing itself with the extensive powers of Chapter VII; where the Council confers a very wide power, as in resolution 678 of 29 November 1990 authorizing the use of force against Iraq to "restore international peace and security in the area"; or where the Council attempts by resolution to determine certain fundamental legal rights and duties. The question of judicial review of Security Council actions has arisen tangentially in cases brought in the ICJ by Libya in 1992 and Bosnia-Herzegovina in 1993, but the Court has not ventured far in this area.[68]

10

EQUALITY AND DOMINANCE
IN THE UNITED NATIONS

The UN Charter enshrines the principle of the sovereign equality of states. The commitment of international organizations during the UN period to the global application of this principle is historically unparalleled. Almost all earlier systems of states contained strong elements of suzerainty and other types of formal or informal relationships of dominance.[69] Many such elements have in fact remained features of international relations in the UN era. Nevertheless, the strength of the commitment to sovereign equality has added legitimacy to attacks on inequality and dominance and has shaped the structure of these relations.

Perceptions of dominance are the stuff of rhetoric and require careful analysis. The complexity of the problem is illustrated (1) by the fact that two states can each perceive the other as dominant; (2) by the phenomenon that some states accused of domination see themselves as essentially anti-imperialistic; and (3) by the way in which accusations of domination can themselves be used by governments as justifications for exerting pressure on other states.

Arguments that the UN system itself is improperly used as an instrument of domination have had continuous currency throughout the history of the organization. In the early years there were repeated accusations, mainly from the USSR and its allies, that the organization as a whole, and the General Assembly in particular, was controlled by the United States. The rise of the Third World majority in the UN General Assembly in the 1960s, and the frequent Soviet support of Third World positions, led to a completely different perception, especially in the United States, of an organization biased against the West. Then, once regular cooperation became established in the Security Council from about 1987, a new perception began to emerge of an activist Security Council dominated by the United States and its

56

Western allies. Some Third World states expressed the fear that the UN might be becoming a cloak for a new form of imperialism. In general, such perceptions of the UN as a whole being dominated by particular states have involved gross oversimplifications.

Each of these perceptions was accompanied by accusations of "double standards," that is, that the UN would act in support of dominant interests but neglect other cases of equal or greater merit. Such accusations were already rife by the time of the Suez crisis.[70] They have persisted ever since and are an almost unavoidable feature of UN politics. In an organization that has to make decisions in matters involving both general principles and harsh realities, substantive consistency is extraordinarily difficult to achieve, even when procedural standards are applied evenly.

Perceptions that the UN is dominated by particular states can have serious consequences. They have led to refusals to make contributions to various parts of the UN budget; to disregard of General Assembly resolutions; and to mixed support for Security Council enforcement initiatives.

The Charter does make some accommodation to hierarchies of power, most notably in the provisions regarding the Permanent Five in the Security Council, and also regarding trusteeship. Inequality, if not hegemony, is a fundamental feature of international life, and it would be remarkable if it were not reflected in the practice of the UN

While past UN practice has not always been premised on the substantive equality of states, it has generally accepted the core idea of equal sovereignty for independent states. In response to the problems of massive human rights violations, endemic civil wars, and failing states, the Security Council has begun to countenance deeper inroads into traditional state prerogatives. The possibility of new forms of dominance emerging under UN auspices is a source of concern to governments in potential target areas.

While the United States has often been seen, particularly since the end of the Cold War, as using the UN as an instrument for its own national purposes, the US experience of the UN in the post–Cold War period suggests that there are problems for the one remaining superpower if it chooses to act in a multilateral framework. The US-UN relationship confronts the United States and other member states with difficult problems of balance. If the United States pursues its objectives through the UN , it risks accusations of dominance, and if it does not it is accused of unilateralism. In 1992–1993 the United States found itself pressed to make heavy commitments to underwrite operations far from home; to meet expectations of leadership even where direct US interests were not at stake; and to engage in the ponderous and frustrating process of trying to reach decisions through complex international negotiations. After initial enthusiasm for "multilateralism," the Clinton administration began in the latter part of 1993 to enunciate a more circumspect approach that laid comparatively more emphasis on the interests of the United States and its close allies and on the need for the peoples of conflict-torn countries to work out their own solutions.[71] The lesson drawn was that a proactive US role was likely to be viewed by some other states as US dominance of the UN , and by many Americans as an excessive burden whose limits needed sharp definition.

11

PEACEFUL CHANGE

A central issue in evaluating the UN has to be its contribution (or otherwise) to the achievement of peaceful change. It was well recognized at the time of the UN's foundation, as it had been during the League of Nations period, that to attempt simply to maintain peace without providing mechanisms for peaceful change was a recipe for immobilism and eventual failure. Bearing in mind the scope of changes in the world since 1945—the process of decolonization, the decline of old powers and the emergence or reemergence of new ones, shifts in the sources and nature of economic power, the rapid development of military technology, the collapse of regimes in eastern Europe and the Soviet Union in 1989–1991—it is striking that many developments that could easily have occasioned major wars did not do so. While by no means all change has been peaceful, a great deal of peaceful change has been achieved. Although the UN does not deserve all the credit for this, it does deserve some.

The general structure of international order embodied by the UN , and some of the principles and rhetoric associated with it, may have played some part in providing a relatively benign framework for changes in ideologies and political systems. Such changes have deep causes unconnected with the UN, but during the Gorbachev era the framework of cooperative international order made it easier for Soviet leaders to downplay ideological division as a governing feature of international relations. In Gorbachev's foreign policy there was a corresponding emphasis on a much increased role for the UN , initiated in his sweeping proposals of September 1987.[72] This emphasis was pursued in some respects by the successor Russian leaders even after the demise of the Gorbachev regime and the USSR in December 1991.[73]

Although much peaceful change has occurred, it is also true that much important change has not been achieved, most notably in the field of international justice between advantaged and disadvantaged, included and marginalized, North and South. The UN has done much to fuel the revolution of rising expectations that has given voice and strength to diverse and sometimes inconsistent demands for global justice. These demands were themselves translated by their proponents into higher standards against which to measure and criticize the UN's performance, especially during the heyday of arguments for a New International Economic Order in the 1970s. Fundamental differences within the international community about these demands (and about the legitimacy of some of them) were not resolved within or outside the UN. The UN has in some limited respects been seen as an obstacle to their realization, but the principal obstacles to peaceful change in this area are so great as to be largely beyond the UN's resources. This point has been increasingly accepted by many Southern and Northern political leaders, and there has been a gradual and limited convergence of views about what the UN can and should do, reflected, for example, in the 1992 Cartagena agreement about the future direction of UNCTAD. Other demands for justice, including in the areas of gender equality and religious freedom, expose sharp differences among states. The UN is constantly implicated in compromises between values of order and of justice, but the system remains weighted toward maintaining order.

12

PROCLAIMING INTERNATIONAL
PRIORITIES AND PRINCIPLES

Despite its various failings, the UN has by no means lost its importance as a proclaimer of international standards. This complex role is
central both to the maintenance of a viable international order and
to the communication, consolidation, and development of shared values within international society.

CHARTER PRINCIPLES

The centerpiece of the UN's proclamation of international principles
and standards remains, even today, the Charter of 1945. The Charter,
or at least the Charter order, proclaims such principles as sovereign
equality; territorial integrity and political independence of states;
equal rights and self-determination of peoples; nonintervention in
internal affairs except under Chapter VII; peaceful settlement of disputes; abstention from threats or uses of force; fulfillment in good
faith of international obligations; international cooperation; and
respect for and promotion of human rights and fundamental free-
doms without discrimination.[74] Inevitably there are differences in
interpretation of these terse statements of principle, which were
drawn up by a limited group of states in a somewhat different world.
Nevertheless, the dominant diplomatic view has been that the
Charter principles are an exemplary basis for the conduct of international relations, and that the need is not to rethink any of them but to
focus, as the UN has done, on elaborating them and developing new
principles where necessary. There are, however, fundamental ten-
sions between some of the principles. For example, as in the case of
Yugoslavia in 1991, the principles of territorial integrity and self-

determination may prove irreconcilable. Equally, as in the cases of many countries subject to international criticism for violations of human rights, the principles of nonintervention and human rights may come into conflict.[75] Where revisionist pressures have become very strong, there has been controversy about relations between values of order and of justice, expressed for instance in debates about the relations of the principles of peaceful settlement and nonuse of force on one hand and human rights and self-determination on the other. There has also been criticism of the state-centric nature of the Charter principles, occasionally because of fundamental dissatisfaction with the Charter scheme as a foundation for global order, but more often with a view to adding further principles directed toward redistributing wealth or power, to empowering nonstate groups (especially "peoples"), or to reorienting priorities toward such issues as developmental or ecological concerns.[76]

Another view of the Charter principles is that they are incorrigibly idealistic. In many ways, however, the Charter is a distinctly hard-headed document.[77] For example, it is extremely cautious in discussing disarmament, and it refers not to the long-asserted but highly problematic principle of "national self-determination," but to the much vaguer formulation "equal rights and self-determination of peoples," which was less haunted by ghosts from Europe's history between the two world wars.[78] To some extent the Charter anticipated the growth of concern with economic and social matters and human rights, the advent of regional security organizations, and the process of decolonization.

In addition to these different interpretations of the Charter's actual provisions, there are different views of its whole ethos. Some, particularly those steeped in constitutionalist domestic polities such as the USA, are inclined to find the solution to questions of all sorts in the interpretation and reinterpretation of Charter provisions. This tendency has often coincided with organic views of an expanding and diversifying UN , founded on an ethos of continuous progress and sustained by teleological interpretations of the original Charter language. The Charter embodies the architecture of a dynamic organization, but it is not a complete constitution for international society. The Charter's foundational principles do not contain prescriptions for all problems of international public order, let alone for all issues of international justice. The UN has thus been concerned both with elaborating existing principles and with formulating new standards, a task it has shared with many other international institutions.

ARTICULATION OF NEW ISSUES

The UN serves an important function in shaping the international agenda and in both facilitating and conditioning the articulation of new political demands. It has contributed to global awareness of numerous issues, including racial discrimination, torture and disappearances, rights of children, illiteracy, international dimensions of poverty, problems relating to refugees, and protection of cultural heritage. It has become deeply involved in a wide range of environmental issues, although this involvement has led to problems of simultaneous and sometimes uncoordinated action in environmental policy by a multitude of UN subsidiary bodies and specialized agencies. In addition, the UN has roles in areas such as improving control of the production, trade, and consumption of narcotics, where international coordination of national policies and actions is more effective if accompanied by collective legitimation of otherwise controversial measures.[79] More generally, UN endorsement lends legitimacy to doctrines and ideas concerning such matters as development assistance, the "common heritage of mankind" in the deep-sea bed and outer space, and the unacceptability of colonialism. UN endorsement may also legitimize compromise solutions reached in particular international disputes and crises.

UN and regional standard-setting instruments and the bodies charged with their implementation have prompted a convergence of the public pronouncements of states in a common international rhetoric of human rights. To a much smaller extent this convergence is mirrored in domestic practice. Despite the existence of many purportedly definitive agreements on the subject, different societies have and will continue to have very different conceptions of the nature, content, and importance of human rights.[80] Nevertheless, the growth in the importance attached to human rights in most states is in significant measure a product of the extensive activity stimulated by the UN : international standards and institutions have provided a basis for domestic human rights activism and resistance to governmental oppression as well as for international pressure.

There are signs, albeit limited, that the UN may be becoming more closely associated with the promotion of multiparty democracy. Since the late 1980s it has been involved in election-monitoring activities in many independent countries, including Nicaragua, Haiti, El Salvador, Angola, Cambodia, and Mozambique. Although several of these operations have related to international peace and security and been undertaken under the auspices of the Security Council, there is also noticeably less opposition in the General Assembly to such activities than in earlier periods. Boutros-Ghali has put great emphasis on democracy and its significance both for economic development and for international peace.[81] The evidence that democratic states have a good record of avoiding war with each other is often adduced to show the relevance of democracy to the peace and security purposes of the UN system.[82]

However, support for and advocacy of democracy need to be tempered by awareness of several major obstacles. Many states continue to emphasize the principle of noninterference in internal affairs and resist pressures to change their systems of government. In some societies, public life and cultural norms are very different from those associated with Western democratic forms. There is in any case no consensus on the universal desirability of particular democratic models. Further, the problems of transition from authoritarian to democratic systems, and of establishing democratic structures in the face of severe communal division, are immense. In some societies the introduction of democratic politics may actually exacerbate already severe ethnic or other divisions, compel people to identify with one community or another, and even lead to the outbreak of war. Developments in several successor states of the former Yugoslavia and the former Soviet Union illustrate some of the hazards. In these and other cases, the introduction of democracy may require much more assistance than the UN and other international agencies can realistically provide, as the postelection problems of Haiti and Angola graphically demonstrate. Nevertheless, the legitimizing effect of prodemocratic incantations and international observation, and such practical contributions as electoral aid and voter education, may well be important for emerging democracies and for vulnerable existing democracies.[83]

PROBLEMS IN UN STANDARD-SETTING

UN standard-setting, while often useful, can be deeply flawed. The necessities of coalition maintenance may lead to incoherent compromises or to the agglomeration of demands in such grand abstractions as the "New World Information and Communication Order."[84] The UN has sometimes been involved in the advocacy of principles that are undefined, contradictory, or essentially and fiercely contested. One of many possible examples is that of the principles that were recognized in the charter and judgment of the International Military Tribunal at Nuremberg in 1945–1946, at which German war criminals were convicted. On 11 December 1946 the UN General Assembly unanimously adopted a brief resolution affirming the Nuremberg principles. Subsequent attempts by the International Law Commission and other bodies to codify these principles did not gain general acceptance, partly because of the resistance of some states to the principle recognizing the legitimacy of disobeying orders from a superior. However, the Statute of the International Tribunal on war crimes in former Yugoslavia, adopted unanimously by the Security Council in May 1993, did contain provisions on superior orders and other key principles.[85]

In many cases the rhetorical declamation of sweeping principles by the UN has clouded judgment, and there are some highly simplistic elements in the ethos of the organization that need to be questioned from within as well as without. To take just one example, the UN increasingly committed itself over the years to the goal of general and complete disarmament, and the General Assembly held Special Sessions on Disarmament in 1978, 1982, and 1988. However, there was little analysis under UN auspices of why ambitious calls for disarmament, which have been a persistent feature of international life since at least 1899, have invariably failed. In particular, the possibility that the idea of general and complete disarmament as commonly proposed may contain some inbuilt defects (rather than merely facing external "obstacles") seldom got a hearing. General and complete disarmament had the character of a myth to which the UN subscribed, rather than an issue that it rigorously analyzed. This approach to disarmament has several possible costs. First, it can contribute to verbal hostility between states as they blame each other for the failure to achieve the goal. Second, by presenting a mythological alternative to armament it may distract attention from other, possibly more fruitful approaches to the urgent problem of controlling and limiting military force—including many approaches in arms control and laws of war matters that the UN has pursued. And third, it risks having the same effect as the League of Nations' commitment to disarmament in the 1920s and 1930s—namely, not just that it will fail to produce results, but that in so doing it will weaken the international organization that committed itself so deeply to this approach.[86] In the post–Cold War era there are signs that the UN , including its Centre for Disarmament Affairs, is taking a less propagandistic view of disarmament, but a coherent vision of the place of arms limitation in international politics has not yet emerged.[87]

Other principles espoused by the UN have also proved problematic in practice. In the post–Cold War era, crises arising from the disintegration of federal states have raised questions about the appropriateness of applying in an undifferentiated way certain vital principles derived from the somewhat different context of interstate relations. The principle that changing frontiers by force can never be accepted is fundamental in contemporary international relations and was immediately invoked by the international community in connection with the Yugoslavia crisis.[88] It was held to be applicable both because of the characterization of the crisis as a conflict between states and because dangerous precedents could be set by successful grabs for territory on largely ethnic grounds. The question remains whether it was wise to express this legal principle so forcefully in the special context of the disintegration of federal states where, as in this case, some of the existing "frontiers" have no physical existence and lack both logic and legitimacy, where there are such deep-seated ethnic problems, and where almost any imaginable outcome short of massive conflagration involves some de facto success for those who seek to change frontiers by force.

The experience of the UN era has shown that there are problems not only in the unequal application of principles in comparable cases but also in attempts to apply the same principles to very different situations, regions, and countries. The nature of a global organization is to seek to develop and apply common standards. The universalizing tendency is continuously confronted with differences: whether between high-technology and low-technology countries in ability to control toxic emissions; between fundamentally different attitudes to the position of women; or between maritime and landlocked countries in ability to exploit freedom of high-seas fishing. The UN has developed numerous exceptions allowing differential application of general principles to developing countries, specially affected states, or states with special needs, and many principles themselves are carefully contextualized.

The UN has had particular difficulty in enunciating effective principles for tackling one of the most basic divisions of international life—the division between the largely affluent societies of the North and the largely poor societies of the South.[89] Conscious of a link between economic disruption and war, those who framed the Charter placed much emphasis on economic and social progress, especially in the preamble and Chapters IX and X. The UN General Assembly began to proclaim an ideology of development, couched increasingly in terms of rights or entitlements, in the mid-1960s. After a long period of virtual silence on the subject, even the Security Council began in the early 1990s to return rhetorically to the connection between development and international peace, although it has little to show in immediate results. In this area, more than in many others, there has been a huge gulf between the UN rhetoric and the progress actually achieved in large parts of the South. Expectations that the UN could play a central role in development issues have had to yield to a more cautious view of the UN's potential capacities and a more nuanced understanding of the nature of the development process. The rhetorical and programmatic UN commitment to development has nevertheless continued, although it has proved increasingly difficult to integrate this commitment with other UN priorities. A long-running debate on the real relations between human rights vis-à-vis the state and state-supervised development has never been effectively resolved beyond superficial agreement on the formula that they are mutually interdependent. The debate on relations between environment and development has similarly produced a verbal commitment to "sustainable development," but without an underlying reconciliation of the very different agendas. The backdrop of the general unwillingness of the North to make the sacrifices necessary to finance the development urged by the South has not changed greatly throughout the UN period, but the UN's treatment of these issues has contributed to improved understanding of them.

LEGITIMATION AND RECOGNITION

Although it has been embroiled in controversy over the principles it espouses, as well as in other areas of its activities, the UN has by no means lost its legitimacy. Nor has it lost its important capacity to confer legitimacy.[90] Participation in UN activities has helped confer legitimacy on new states that might otherwise be uncertain of their international status; on particular regimes within states; and on certain nonstate entities, such as the Palestine Liberation Organization (PLO) and the South West Africa People's Organization (SWAPO).[91]

The UN has an important role in the matter of recognition of states and governments. Its record is far from perfect—witness the exclusion of communist China from the UN from 1949 to 1971. However, the considerable (though by no means total) agreement about what states exist, and what governments represent those states, is due in part to the role of the UN as an intergovernmental body that admits (or refuses to admit) states as members and examines the credentials of the representatives of those states. When the UN admits member states, it is not only conferring recognition on them but also implicitly giving them a kind of guarantee against external attack.

The traditional criteria for recognition of new states include consideration of whether a state really exists and is capable of entering into and honoring commitments on a long-term basis. In the recognition and admission of postcolonial states for much of the period after 1945, there was a strong tendency to accept states established by agreement within the former colonial boundaries, even if their political cohesion and economic viability was not absolutely assured. The viability of new and vulnerable states was buttressed by the norm of nonrevision of former colonial boundaries, and restraints on intervention. However, the disintegration of the long-established federal states of the Soviet Union and Yugoslavia in 1991–1992 raised special problems in the creation of new states. The international community's view that the internal boundaries of the former federations should provide the basis for the emergence and identity of any new states proved difficult to maintain effectively in several cases. In attempting to maintain peace during the disintegration of Yugoslavia, the UN and its members recognized successor states, including Croatia and Bosnia-Herzegovina, despite the absence of effective multilateral or bilateral arrangements to ensure their viability in the face of evident internal and external challenges.[92] In such cases, premature acts of recognition risk dragging the UN even further into costly ethnic and territorial conflicts.

THE NEED FOR IMPLEMENTATION OF STANDARDS

The UN's functions in proclaiming principles and conferring legitimacy remain central to the effective maintenance of international society. If international society is to develop further, however, a much greater emphasis on effective implementation of standards must be the highest priority.[93] As Sir Frank Berman puts it:

> It seems to many that the problem is not to discover what the law is, or how to apply it to the particular case, or even whether the existing rule is "satisfactory" or not, but rather how to secure or compel compliance with the law at all. It may be that we have now passed from a great phase of new law-making to a period where the focus is not on new substantive law but on how to make existing law more effective.[94]

In many cases, state structures and national legal systems remain the most effective means of implementing international norms (arguments for supranationality notwithstanding). The breakdown of domestic order and domestic rule of law systems is one of the most serious threats to the effectiveness of international law.

There are many difficulties in making existing international law—or at least certain key parts of it—more effective. The central difficulties arise in cases where particular states are themselves opposed to international norms or are unwilling or unable to exert control over certain nonstate groups involved in such acts as piracy, drug-running, war crimes, and terrorism.

In some such cases—whether alleged terrorists in Libya or war crimes in former Yugoslavia—the UN has sought to impose basic and important international legal standards through trials of individuals outside the states concerned. The moral and legal logic of establishing the International Tribunal on war crimes in former Yugoslavia is impressive, and the demonstration effect may have lasting significance. However, the practical problems are severe: how to secure the arrest and extradition of suspects and how to maintain demands for trials of certain leaders when those leaders are also needed to negotiate a military or political settlement. The risk is that such legal approaches will run up against the obstinacy and power of sovereign states: law (and with it, the UN) may be shown to lack teeth and to have become too far removed from the facts of power.

13

PROBLEMS OF INSTITUTIONAL ETHOS

Although the UN has considerable achievements to its credit, it also has ingrained faults—not least in its institutional ethos and its organizational structure. Some of these faults have adversely affected its performance: indeed, the UN can at times exacerbate the problems it is intended to ameliorate.

The faults of the institutional ethos have been of several kinds. The long-established diplomatic practice of using verbal formulae to conceal real differences has flourished to excess in the UN framework. The equally ancient habit of resorting to rhetorical approaches to complex problems has also had a prominent place in the General Assembly and in many other parts of the system. Such styles of discourse can cloud analysis and hamper effective decisionmaking. There has been a tendency to sententious proclamation that exaggerates the importance of resolutions and texts at the expense of serious consideration of the substantive realities. Especially in the Security Council, but elsewhere as well, there has been occasional evidence of isolation from reality: participants have sometimes appeared to assume that what is solemnly resolved in New York is capable of being, and actually will be, transformed into effective action.

Within the UN system there has not been a tradition of reflective debate about the organization's overall place in international relations, and the contribution of the academic community to major UN debates has been relatively limited. Analysis of the UN has often been impaired by temporal parochialism, in which the past is simplified or seen as irrelevant. The UN system has also been characterized by a parochial form of internationalism, employing rhetoric suggesting that all peoples and countries think alike and share the same concerns and the same interests, when the practical experience of the organization has frequently testified to the contrary. Similarly, there has often been blithe disregard in the face of well-founded or politically damning criticism.

14

THE UNITED NATIONS IN THE
FIRMAMENT OF INTERNATIONAL RELATIONS

The roles of the UN must not be assessed in isolation from other aspects of international relations. Part of the genius of the Charter order is precisely the integration of the UN into the wider structure of the international system.[95] Proposals for change are likely to run into difficulty if they do not take this central fact into account.

The ancient institutions of diplomacy and balance of power, operating only slightly differently in the UN era, remain fundamental features of the international system. Over centuries, states have devised numerous means of harmonizing their interests, mitigating their conflicts, or at least preventing disputes from leading to total war. True, these means have been far from perfect—witness the outbreak of two world wars in this century. But many of the functions that the UN performs can be—and sometimes are—performed by other entities as well. Though the UN has mediated some disputes, it is also true that in other conflicts other mediators or arbitrators have been used: for example, in 1979–1984 it was papal mediation that settled the long-standing Beagle Channel dispute between Argentina and Chile.[96] UN peacekeeping forces have been used in some conflicts, but non-UN forces have helped settle other long-standing problems: for example, Commonwealth forces monitored the elections and transfer of power in Zimbabwe in 1980 following the Lancaster House agreement of the previous year. Although the UN has contributed notably to the development of international law, it is also true that this body of law is very much older than the UN , is well rooted in the overlapping interests of states, develops outside as well as within UN auspices, and would continue to exist even if the UN were to disappear tomorrow.[97] The UN has made some progress in proclaiming human rights standards and in seeing to their implementation, but greater protection has been provided in many individual states and by regional groupings—for example, through the 1950 European Convention on Human Rights and the commission and court established under it. Though states have on occasion paid a high political price for ignoring UN principles and procedures, in other cases the political restraints on state behavior have operated quite independently of the UN.

Many states and groups of states have achieved a degree of stability in their international relations by means that do not depend on the UN but that are compatible with (and even foreseen by) the UN system. Many governments rely on their individual or collective possession of military power rather than on any benign UN framework.

The UN era has also been characterized by the development of a remarkable variety of regional and subregional organizations of a political, economic, or military character. Chapter VIII of the UN Charter envisaged a significant place for such organizations, but in fact their roles have been disparate. Reasons for using regional organizations in handling disputes include participation by local powers, burden-sharing, relief of UN overload, and avoidance of controversial involvement of extraregional powers. Possible drawbacks include local hegemony; lack of regional cooperation and resources; proximity creating vulnerability; and a multiplicity of possible organizations in a single region, with consequent problems of choice, rivalry, and confusion. Regional organizations may well take on greater roles, as Boutros-Ghali has urged, but in most cases they lack the requisite political and operational capability, and there is little prospect that they will supplant the role of the UN .[98]

Over the course of its first half century, the UN has become an established part of the firmament of international relations. It is involved in a vast range of activities, many of them central to the functioning of international society. The UN is best seen not as a vehicle for completely restructuring or replacing the system of sovereign states but as ameliorating the problems spawned by that system's imperfections and as managing processes of rapid change in many distinct fields. The UN finds roles in areas of activity that are most appropriately tackled either on a truly multilateral basis or by individuals representing not a particular state but a collectivity of states. To the extent that the UN is involved in the transformation of international society, it is not by creating a new and conceptually simple supranational structure but by a more general process whereby management of different problems is allocated to different, albeit overlapping and fluctuating, levels.

Now that the UN has emerged from the Cold War, and the Security Council in particular is much more capable of reaching decisions than before, the UN system is developing as a unique combination of two elements: on one hand, a genuinely global organization with near-universal membership; on the other, something like a Concert of Powers in the Security Council, managing international security affairs in a way that inevitably reflects the preoccupations of its leading members (not least the United States) and is inevitably resented by states that feel left out of the decisionmaking.

15

CONCLUSION: SOME PROPOSITIONS ON CHANGE IN THE UNITED NATIONS

This paper has the central purpose not of advancing particular proposals for change but of suggesting a possible framework for understanding the UN's place in international relations. It has attempted an exploration of how to think about the UN , whose place in international relations has proved different from that envisaged both by advocates and by critics. It has sought to move away from the pietistic tradition in the study of international organizations, and from the tradition that emphasizes prescription with little examination of what already exists. It has sought to evaluate the UN's performance against a modest yardstick rather than an impossible ideal. Nonetheless, some propositions regarding the way that proposals for UN change in the post–Cold War era should be considered do emerge from this analysis:

1. The UN is a unique entity, very different from the states of which it is composed. It has developed its own character, areas of activity, and methods of operation. Its powers and capacities are considerable, varied, and sometimes in tension with each other, but they are not those of a government. There is no prospect of the UN becoming a supranational government in relation to states.

2. The key issue is not to "strengthen the UN" in the simple sense of giving it more autonomy, a more governmental character, or more independent control of military power. While the UN undeniably needs strengthening in certain respects, in most of its activities it must necessarily continue to operate in conjunction with states.

3. The factors that enablinged the UN to develop in its first half century, as the first global political organization with virtually universal membership, are more complex than is often suggested. The UN is frequently seen as having proved more successful and enduring than its predecessor, the League of Nations, because it has more

power both to make and to implement decisions and therefore has more "muscle." While there is truth in this notion, the relative success of the UN system owes much to the fact that its Charter was designed to accommodate the UN in the system of states rather than to pose a direct challenge to that system, as its predecessor's Covenant did. The League Covenant was in many respects (disarmament, obligations to take part in collective security, the requirements to submit disputes to arbitration) a more explicit challenge to the rights of states than the Charter. The UN owes some of its effectiveness to going with rather than against the grain of the system of states.

4. Consideration of the UN's roles should not be based on a presupposition that these roles were entirely negative during the Cold War years. There was merit in certain approaches of that time, including the maintenance of the UN's near-universal character, the recognition of deep divisions in matters of ideology and foreign policy, the acceptance that not all problems could be tackled in a UN framework, and the emphasis on aspirational pronouncements and standards. Such approaches need to be adapted to the circumstances of a new era but should not simply be abandoned on the erroneous assumption that international society is now totally transformed. For better or for worse, many elements of the system that operated during the Cold War, including the tendency of major powers to handle their mutual conflicts largely outside the UN framework, show signs of continuing.

5. The UN faces special hazards as well as opportunities in the post–Cold War era. It is required to address a wider and more taxing range of problems than ever before, it has an enhanced capacity to make decisions on action concerning these problems, and it can no longer use the Cold War divide as an all-purpose exculpation for its numerous failures to take effective action.

6. One problem of the post–Cold War order is that the UN is widely seen as the instrument of the one remaining superpower and as having moved from being paralyzed to being led by the nose. Such a perception is an inaccurate reflection of the complexities of UN diplomacy and decisionmaking. Acting through the UN may be the only or best alternative for the United States on many issues, but it is likely to have costs. Multilateral decisionmaking is frequently complicated and inconclusive and liable to produce a series of incoherent compromises. Commitment to the UN brings a member state valuable allies and political support on particular issues and may well contribute to the broader stability of the international system, but it also leads to a degree of entanglement that may propel states into involvements they might otherwise prefer to evade.

7. If the United States defines its national interest in the UN too narrowly, or sets so many preconditions upon its commitment of any US troops to UN operations as to make its meaningful participation rare, the United States may so restrict its options for containing particular conflicts as to have none that are capable of producing satisfactory results. This risk is exacerbated by policies of severe financial stringency toward UN operations.

8. The window of opportunity to build patterns of cooperation, or at least acquiescence, among major powers may exist for only a short period. Much may be gained by maximum use of this opportunity to develop and embed techniques of cooperation, inclusion, joint action, and accommodation of mutual interests in ways that may endure future periods of tension.

9. The UN needs to avoid becoming the convenient repository for the most difficult problems of international relations, including civil wars. It cannot be assumed that an international organization will necessarily be more successful than states in tackling problems of a perennially difficult character. States tend to address manageable problems themselves and to transfer unmanageable ones to other bodies. The UN is likely to need means of avoiding intractable or excessively risky commitments, and for all its faults the veto system may continue to provide one such mechanism.

10. It is probably a mistake to characterize the system of security that has developed in the UN era as one of collective security, even in embryo. The end of the Cold War and the enhanced possibilities for the Security Council reaching effective decisions have undoubtedly enlarged the sphere of multilateral military action, at least for the time being, but that is not the same thing as creating a global system of collective security. Progress has been limited because of the continued existence of factors that have bedeviled efforts at collective security in the past. Advocacy of collective security in the post–Cold War era has not adequately addressed the well-known problems associated with the idea.

11. The character of UN peacekeeping operations has unavoidably become increasingly varied, even to the point where actions of fundamentally different kinds are subsumed under the same label. Peacekeeping efforts have traditionally operated mainly in situations where the parties were broadly willing to accept them and had an interest in a measure of peace, if not permanent settlement of the conflict. The various forms of this traditional UN peacekeeping have been important and much acclaimed. The UN has increasingly been drawn into other situations where the element of consent is much reduced or lacking and where "peacekeeping" involves trying to

impose peace as well as trying to keep it. It will not be possible, nor even desirable, to return to a world in which UN peacekeeping in all circumstances depends on consent of all parties to a conflict. The challenge is to develop practice concerning mandates, planning, operational capacity, management, control, accountability, and political support for UN forces that meets the new exigencies while retaining to the greatest extent possible the qualities and principles that have contributed so notably to the reputation and effectiveness of traditional UN forces.

12. A succession of crises, including many in the field of peacekeeping, has exposed severe problems regarding the methods of pressure used by the UN. Attempts to implement the will of the Security Council against tough adversaries with strong local support are fraught with difficulty. There is a strong possibility that in such situations the UN may rely heavily on a range of coercive methods intended to minimize UN casualties, including sanctions, sophisticated military interventions, and even (despite some reluctance) the threat or use of bombing. Such methods are on occasion necessary, but they are blunt instruments: they risk alienating international and local opinion and do not always offer prospects of gaining real control or lasting influence in a country.

13. While the UN is right to focus on the importance of universal standards to which its member states are subject, it must be cautious and selective about getting involved in head-on clashes with member states on these matters. If the UN publicly makes concrete demands regarding the observance of particular norms but lacks the means of enforcing such demands, it may not only expose its own weakness but also risk weakening the very norms it seeks to strengthen. Uncoordinated international attempts to insist upon compliance with a plethora of standards—particularly by formal or informal imposition of conditions relating to matters as diverse as human rights, multiparty democracy, good governance, defense spending, arms sales, agricultural pricing, and environmental emissions—may degenerate into conflicting prescriptions, incoherent priorities, and outraged citizenry.

14. The UN does have a capacity to set aspirational standards and to draw on its prestige and aura of standing above governments in order to achieve more than its material power and resources would otherwise allow. In these respects it does shape the values and behavior of states and individuals, and curb some of their excesses. But this capacity to influence beyond its material power is not unlimited, and the credibility of the UN is jeopardized when its rhetoric and espe-

cially its attempted actions go too far beyond its real resources. Decisionmakers in the UN need to carefully evaluate the influence that the UN can exert in each case, and weigh the price of failure along with the returns of success.

15. The UN has gone some way to accommodate the roles of non-state activities and nongovernmental organizations in international relations, though as an intergovernmental organization its adaptation to their increasing roles is likely to remain slow.

16. The UN's parlous financial situation has been and remains an obstacle to the organization's effectiveness. While financial stringency has been a means of stimulating reform, the failure by many states to pay their dues has also had the greater effect of inhibiting planning and results-oriented management. The sums of money involved, although growing, are still comparatively modest. In the absence of a creative new approach to funding the UN , it is urgent that the major states make a serious political commitment to paying their dues in timely fashion and to placing UN finances on a more satisfactory long-term basis.

17. As to the UN's organizational structure and formal proce-dures, the urgency of reform is now widely acknowledged, and there remain pressing needs for streamlining and rationalization within and beyond the UN system. The UN has a successful if unexciting his-tory of evolution and will certainly need to change further to meet its wide range of responsibilities. Adaptation and change in organiza-tional structures, in procedures, and in practices is an organic process. It involves responding pragmatically, with elements of prece-dent and common law, to problems for which old frameworks or approaches are inadequate. Many such changes have not come under the crusading banner of "reform."

18. Reform of the Security Council has become an especially pressing question because the Council is, for the time being at least, able to play a significant role in some security issues. The Council is required to make difficult decisions about which problems to address, which actions to take, and which problems to evade. If decisions on such matters are to have a chance of commanding legitimacy and securing effective support, wider participation in the decisionmaking process is essential. An increase in the membership of the Council would require Charter revisions that will be difficult but not necessar-ily impossible to achieve. Such an increase must not render the Council unwieldy and incapable of effective action. The proposals for formal change most likely to command the necessary support include a small increase in permanent members (perhpas as few as two), pos-

sibly without the veto, and a somewhat larger increase in the number of nonpermanent members, with some relaxation in the rules that presently prevent reelection following a two-year term.

19. Any vision of the UN's future should focus on areas in which the UN has, at least potentially, a comparative advantage over states acting unilaterally or in other ways, and also over nongovernmental bodies. In many such areas a global consensus on policy and values is fundamental to effective action: protection of the global climate system; maintenance of a high-seas regime; resolution of coordination problems of global communications; control or eradication of diseases; development of population policies and programs; elaboration of a degree of shared responsibility for such goals as sustainable development; maintenance and implementation of minimum standards of human rights; and delivery of humanitarian assistance and disaster relief. There are also areas in which the UN's prestige, detachment, and experience are valuable assets: peacekeeping, election observation and supervision, human rights monitoring, and dispute settlement. This vision, rather than that of an aspiring world government, is the more appropriate one in the present state of international society.

*   *   *

"The tents have been struck, and the great caravan of humanity is once more on the march." So said Jan Christian Smuts in 1918, at the time of the planning of the League of Nations.[99] It is tempting to dismiss such views as part of the inflated rhetoric that international organizations seem so often to attract. But in our still divided world, there remains a need for an institution that can in some way, however imperfectly, articulate the twin ideas of a universal society of states and the cosmopolitan universality of humankind.

NOTES

1. On usage of the term *anarchy* in academic writing on international relations, see Hedley Bull, *The Anarchical Society: A Study of Order in World Politics* (London, 1977); Kenneth Waltz, *Theory of International Politics* (Reading, Mass., 1979); Arthur Stein, "Coordination and Collaboration: Regimes in an Anarchic World," *International Organization* 36 (1982), pp. 294–324; Kenneth Oye (ed.), *Cooperation Under Anarchy* (Princeton, 1986); Helen Milner, "The Assumption of Anarchy in International Relations Theory: A Critique," *Review of International Studies* 17 (1991), pp. 67–85; and David Baldwin (ed.), *Neorealism and Neoliberalism: The Contemporary Debate* (New York, 1993).

2. The concept of a global international society is examined in Hedley Bull, *The Anarchical Society;* and Hedley Bull and Adam Watson (eds.), *The Expansion of International Society* (Oxford, 1984).

3. An important study was Robert Keohane and Joseph Nye (eds.), *Transnational Relations and World Politics* (Cambridge, Mass., 1972). On the role of epistemic communities, see Peter Haas (ed.), "Knowledge, Power and International Policy Coordination," *International Organization* 46 (Winter 1992).

4. See generally James N. Rosenau and Ernst-Otto Czempiel (eds.), *Governance Without Government: Order and Change in World Politics* (Cambridge, 1992); M. J. Peterson, "Transnational Activity, International Society and World Politics," *Millennium* 21 (1992), pp. 371–388; and Anne-Marie Slaughter Burley, "International Law and International Relations Theory: A Dual Agenda," *American Journal of International Law* 87 (1993), pp. 205–239.

5. On sovereignty, see R. B. J. Walker, *Inside/Outside: International Relations as Political Theory* (Cambridge, 1993). On territoriality and sovereignty, see John Gerard Ruggie, "Territoriality and Beyond," *International Organization* 47 (1993), pp. 139–174. A wide-ranging presentation of these perspectives is Ronnie D. Lipschutz and Ken Conca (eds.), *The State and Social Power in Global Environmental Politics* (New York, 1993). Cf. Immanuel Wallerstein, *Geopolitics and Geoculture: Essays on the Changing World System* (Cambridge, 1991).

6. See, e.g., Carl Kaysen, "Is War Obsolete?" *International Security* 14 (1990), pp. 42–64.

7. Samuel P. Huntington, "The Clash of Civilizations?" *Foreign Affairs* 72 (Summer 1993), p. 22.

8. The pattern of vision and disillusion in the history of proposals for international organizations to maintain peace is traced in F. H. Hinsley, *Power and the Pursuit of Peace* (Cambridge, 1963). See also J. Ter Meulen, *Der Gedanke der internationalen Organisation in seiner Entwicklung*, 2 vols. (The Hague, 1917, 1929).

9. Boutros Boutros-Ghali, *An Agenda for Peace: Preventive Diplomacy, Peacemaking and Peace-keeping* (United Nations, New York, 1992). See also "Implementation of the Recommendations Contained in 'An Agenda for Peace,'" UN doc. A/47/965 of 15 June 1993.

10. See, e.g., the thoughtful book by Australian Foreign Minister Gareth Evans, *Cooperating for Peace: The Global Agenda for the 1990s and Beyond* (New South Wales, 1993).

11. The Washington Declaration, the Moscow Declaration, and other instruments of the wartime United Nations are conveniently reprinted in Royal Institute of International Affairs, *United Nations Documents 1941–1945* (London, 1946); and in Louise W. Holborn, *War and Peace Aims of the United Nations*, 2 vols. (Boston, 1943, 1948).

12. The term *UN system* refers not just to the United Nations itself, as outlined in the Charter, but also to the various subsidiary bodies and specialized agencies that operate under its auspices.

13. The importance of symbolic resolutions to coalition maintenance within the UN is demonstrated by M. J. Peterson, *The General Assembly in World Politics* (Boston, 1986), pp. 187ff.

14. The UN Charter provision for unanimity among the Permanent Members of the Security Council (the veto) was the result of extensive discussion, including at Dumbarton Oaks (Aug.–Oct. 1944) and Yalta (Feb. 1945). The evidence is that the UK, United States, USSR, and France all favored the principle of unanimity and that they were motivated in this by a hardheaded concern to protect their own sovereign rights and national interests. See, e.g., Winston S. Churchill, *The Second World War*, vol. 6, *Triumph and Tragedy* (London, 1954), pp. 181–182 and 308–313; Harry S Truman, *Year of Decisions: 1945* (London, 1955), pp. 194–195, 201, and 206–207; Charles de Gaulle, *War Memoirs: Salvation 1944–1946—Documents*, trans. Murchie and Erskine (London, 1960), pp. 94–95. Truman, who became president of the United States in April 1945, went so far as to write in his memoirs: "All our experts, civil and military, favoured it, and without such a veto no arrangement would have passed the Senate" (p. 207).

15. This table is based on information in Foreign and Commonwealth Office, Research and Analysis Department memorandum, "Table of Vetoed Draft Resolutions in the United Nations Security Council 1946–1991," London, Jan. 1992. There are complexities in determining what constitutes a vetoed resolution, leading to discrepancies between sources due to use of different criteria. Russia succeeded the USSR with effect from 24 December 1991.

16. On the sixteen specialized agencies, see David Pitt and Thomas G. Weiss (eds.), *The Nature of United Nations Bureaucracies* (London, 1986); and Douglas Williams, *The Specialized Agencies and the United Nations: The System in Crisis* (London, 1987).

17. Figures from *Financing an Effective United Nations: A Report of the*

Independent Advisory Group on U.N. Financing (Ford Foundation, New York, 1993), pp. 8 and 30. The US is the largest debtor. In his address to the UN General Assembly on 27 September 1993, President Clinton announced a plan for phased payment of this US debt, while also calling for an eventual reduction in the percentage of UN assessments borne by the United States. President Clinton had continuing difficulty, however, in securing Congressional support for full payment of debts to the UN.

    18. See, e.g., Clyde Eagleton, *International Government*, 3d rev. ed. (New York, 1957).

    19. See, e.g., Daniel Patrick Moynihan, *A Dangerous Place* (London, 1979); and Burton Yale Pines (ed.), *A World Without a UN: What Would Happen If the UN Shut Down?* (Heritage Foundation, Washington, DC, 1984).

    20. The relationship between these two approaches in the US debate is cogently analyzed by Thomas M. Franck, *Nation Against Nation: What Happened to the UN Dream and What the US Can Do About It* (New York, 1985).

    21. On the problems of false analogies between the principles that sustain order within states and those of international society, see Hidemi Suganami, *The Domestic Analogy and World Order Proposals* (Cambridge, 1989).

    22. Examples of the balance-sheet approach include G. Niemeyer, "The Balance-Sheet of the League Experiment," *International Organization* 6 (1952), pp. 537–558; Sir Alexander Cadogan, "The United Nations: A Balance Sheet," *Year Book of World Affairs* 5 (1951), pp. 1–11; and Juliana G. Pilon, *The United States and the United Nations: A Balance Sheet* (Heritage Foundation, Washington, DC, 1982).

    23. Cited in *Harvard International Law Journal* 17 (1976), p. 606.

    24. The most substantial and methodologically rigorous work on the impact of international institutions on state behavior has come from regime theory and related work on international cooperation. The category of "regimes" is broader than formal international institutions, encompassing "sets of implicit or explicit principles, norms, rules, and decision-making procedures around which actors' expectations converge." See Stephen Krasner (ed.), *International Regimes* (Ithaca, NY, 1992), p. 2. Partly because much of this work has focused on particular issue areas, the performance of the UN itself has received surprisingly little attention. For a penetrating statement of the neoliberal institutionalist perspective, see Robert O. Keohane, *International Institutions and State Power: Essays in International Relations Theory* (Boulder, Colo., 1989). Work on international cooperation has begun to pay more attention to issues of compliance and enforcement: see, e.g., Oran Young, "On the Effectiveness of International Institutions," in Rosenau and Czempiel (eds.), *Governance Without Government*. For a wider perspective on international institutions in a multilateral system, see John Gerard Ruggie et al., "Symposium: Multilateralism," *International Organization* 46 (Summer 1992).

    25. In addition to UN archives, several other archives have been established to supplement the official records and published memoirs in these respects, including through memoranda, diaries, letters, and interviews with people concerned with episodes of UN history. Examples are the collection of the Yale Institution for Social and Policy Studies; the UN Career Records Project, established in the Western Manuscripts Department of the Bodleian

Library, Oxford, in 1992; and the project set up in Copenhagen in 1992 by the Nordic Association of Former International Civil Servants.

26. For a useful assessment, see F. P. Walters, *A History of the League of Nations* (Oxford, 1960).

27. President de Gaulle of France, as committed to country as he was dismissive of international organizations, spoke of the UN as "les nations dites unies"—the said-to-be-united nations.

28. On the difference between nation and state see Hugh Seton-Watson, *Nations and States* (London, 1977). See also Benedict Anderson, *Imagined Communities: Reflections on the Origin and Spread of Nationalism* (London, 1983); José de Obieta Chalbaud, *El derecho humano de la autodeterminación de los pueblos* (Madrid, 1985); Anthony D. Smith, *The Ethnic Origins of Nations* (Oxford, 1986); and Daniel Patrick Moynihan, *Pandaemonium: Ethnicity in International Politics* (Oxford, 1993).

29. Conor Cruise O'Brien, *The United Nations: Sacred Drama* (London, 1968), p. 11. The theatrical metaphor was also used by Hernane Tavares de Sá, *The Play Within a Play: The Inside Story of the UN* (New York, 1966).

30. On Lie's and Hammarskjöld's difficulties with the USSR, see Brian Urquhart, *Hammarskjöld* (New York, 1972), pp. 456–472; and Urquhart, *Ralph Bunche: An American Life* (New York, 1993), pp. 335–337.

31. See Seymour M. Finger and Arnold A. Saltzman, *Bending with the Winds: Kurt Waldheim and the United Nations* (New York, 1990).

32. See generally Shirley Hazzard, *Defeat of an Ideal: A Study of the Self-Destruction of the United Nations* (Boston, 1973).

33. See M. Virally on Art. 2(4) and A. Cassese on Art. 51, in J.-P. Cot and A. Pellet (eds.), *La Charte des Nations Unies*, 2d ed. (Paris, 1991), pp. 115–128, 771–795. The relationship between rhetoric and practice is also examined in Hedley Bull (ed.), *Intervention in World Politics* (Oxford, 1984), pp. 186–195.

34. UN practice also evinces doubt about the legitimacy of large-scale uses of force by states in other countries, especially against internal rebellion, even when an invitation has been issued by the government concerned. See Louise Doswald-Beck, "The Legal Validity of Military Intervention by Invitation of the Government," *British Year Book of International Law 1985*, pp. 198–252.

35. Although the so-called Kissinger doctrine did foreshadow the possibility of intervention to protect supplies vital to Western security, no such intervention ensued, at least until the exceptional naval involvements in the Gulf in 1987 and then the UN-authorized coalition action in 1991–1992. These actions occurred in much-changed circumstances.

36. See, e.g., GA Res. 34/22 of 14 Nov. 1979 on Cambodia; and GA Res. 2 (ES-VI) of 14 Jan. 1980 on Afghanistan. On the relative impartiality of General Assembly criticism of users of force, see Franck, *Nation Against Nation*, pp. 224–231.

37. The armed intervention in Grenada was deplored as "a flagrant violation of international law" in GA Res. 38/7 of 2 Nov. 1983; the invasion of Panama was similarly deplored in GA Res. 44/240 of 29 Dec. 1989.

38. Questions related to the use of force by nonstate groups are discussed in John Norton Moore (ed.), *Law and Civil War in the Modern World* (Baltimore, 1974); Michael Bothe, Karl Partsch, and Waldemar Solf, *New Rules for Victims of Armed Conflicts: Commentary on the Two 1977 Protocols Additional to the Geneva Conventions of 1949* (The Hague, 1982), pp. 36–52 and

232–258; and Michel Veuthey, *Guérilla et Droit Humanitaire*, 2d ed. (Geneva, 1983).

39. For an account of Soviet doctrines and activities, see Neil MacFarlane, *Superpower Rivalry and Third World Radicalism: The Idea of National Liberation* (Baltimore, 1985). For one of the final expositions of the "Reagan doctrine," which affirmed the legitimacy of US support for an insurgency against a dictatorial government that depends on external support, see Constantine C. Menges, *The Twilight Struggle: The Soviet Union v. the United States Today* (Washington, DC, 1990).

40. Annexed to GA Res. 2625 (XXV) of 24 Oct. 1970.

41. Annexed to GA Res. 3314 (XXIX) of 14 Dec. 1974. See esp. Arts. 3(g) and 7. A parallel tension regarding self-determination is evident in the Declaration of the 1993 World Conference on Human Rights in Vienna.

42. GA Res. 3237 (XXIX) of 22 Nov. 1974. Already on 13 Nov. 1974 the PLO Chairman, Yasser Arafat, had addressed the UN General Assembly; with the exception of Pope Paul in 1965, he was the first such person not representing the government of a UN member state to do so.

43. See, e.g., Moynihan, *A Dangerous Place*, pp. 181–205.

44. GA Res. 3379 (XXX) of 10 Nov. 1975. Revoked by GA Res. 46/86 of 16 Dec. 1991.

45. UN efforts to achieve consensus on aspects of terrorism include GA Res. 3166 (XXVIII) of 14 Dec. 1973, adopting the text of the 1973 Convention on the Protection and Punishment of Crimes Against Internationally Protected Persons, including diplomatic agents (which entered into force on 20 Feb. 1977); GA Res. 34/146 of 17 Dec. 1979, approving the text of the 1979 International Convention Against the Taking of Hostages (which entered into force on 3 June 1983); and GA Res. 40/61 of 9 Dec. 1985, which "condemns as criminal all acts, methods and practices of terrorism wherever and by whomever committed."

46. Speech by Vernon Walters, US Ambassador to the UN, on 15 Apr. 1986 during a debate in the UN Security Council. On 21 Apr. 1986, France, the UK, and the United States vetoed a draft resolution that would have condemned the armed attack on Libya by the United States. *UN Chronicle* (New York) 23, 4 (Aug. 1986), pp. 46–47. See also Abraham D. Sofaer, legal adviser to the US State Department, "Terrorism and the Law," *Foreign Affairs* 64 (1986), pp. 921–922.

47. On the recurrence of collective security practices and proposals over the centuries see Martin Wight, *Systems of States* (Leicester, 1977), pp. 62 and 149–150; and Hinsley, *Power and the Pursuit of Peace*.

48. For an excellent enumeration of questions relating to collective security systems, see Andrew Hurrell, "Collective Security and International Order Revisited," *International Relations* (London) 11, 1 (Apr. 1992), pp. 37–55. See also Leon Gordenker and Thomas G. Weiss, "The Collective Security Idea and Changing World Politics," in Weiss (ed.), *Collective Security in a Changing World* (Boulder, Colo., 1993), pp. 3–18; and R. N. Stromberg, "The Idea of Collective Security," *Journal of the History of Ideas* 17 (1956), p. 251.

49. See, e.g., Fernand van Langenhove, *La Crise du système de sécurité collective des Nations Unies 1946–57* (The Hague, 1958).

50. Recent examinations of continuity and change in UN peacekeeping include F. T. Liu, *United Nations Peacekeeping and the Non-Use of Force* (Boulder,

Colo.: International Peace Academy Occasional Paper, 1992); Marrack Goulding, Under Secretary–General for Political Affairs, in his Cyril Foster Lecture at Oxford University, 4 Mar. 1993, "The Evolution of United Nations Peacekeeping," *International Affairs* 69, 3 (July 1993), pp. 453–455; Mats Berdal, *Whither UN Peacekeeping?* (IISS Adelphi Paper 281, London, October 1993); and Sally Morphet, "UN Peacekeeping and Election Monitoring," in Roberts and Kingsbury (eds.), *United Nations, Divided World,* 2d ed. (Oxford, 1993), pp. 183–239.

51. See Peter Lyon, "The Rise and Fall and Possible Revival of International Trusteeship," *Journal of Commonwealth and Comparative Politics* 31 (March 1993), pp. 96–110.

52. *Agenda for Peace,* para. 21.

53. See generally Margaret Doxey, *International Sanctions in Contemporary Perspective* (London, 1987); David Leyton-Brown (ed.), *The Utility of Economic Sanctions* (New York, 1987); David A. Baldwin, *Economic Statecraft* (Princeton, 1985); Barry E. Carter, *International Economic Sanctions: Improving the Haphazard US Legal Regime* (Cambridge, 1988); Gary Hufbauer et al., *Economic Sanctions Reconsidered* (Washington, DC, 1990); and Patrick Clawson, "Sanctions as Punishment, Enforcement, and Prelude to Further Action," *Ethics and International Affairs* (New York) 7 (1993), pp. 17–37.

54. See SC Res. 83 of 27 June 1950, recommending that member states "furnish such assistance to the Republic of Korea as may be necessary to repel the armed attack and to restore international peace and security in the area"; SC Res. 678 of 29 Nov. 1990, authorizing member states cooperating with the government of Kuwait "to use all necessary means to uphold and implement resolution 660 and all subsequent relevant resolutions and to restore international peace and security in the area"; and SC Res. 794 of 3 December 1992 authorizing the Secretary-General, the United States, and cooperating states "to use all necessary means to establish as soon as possible a secure environment for humanitarian relief operations in Somalia."

55. See the letter of the Secretary-General to the Secretary-General of NATO dated 6 Feb. 1994, annexed to UN doc. S/1994/131, and the letter of the Secretary-General to the President of the Security Council dated 10 Feb. 1994. SC Res. 836 of 4 June 1993 authorized UNPROFOR to use force in self-defense in reply to bombardments against the safe areas declared in SC Res. 824 of 6 May 1993. However, as noted above, SC Res. 836 also authorized the use of force by member states without an unequivocal statement that such uses of force could only be at the express request of UN officials. In Res. 816 of 31 March 1993 the Security Council authorized member states to take all necessary measures to ensure compliance with the Bosnian no-fly zone proclaimed by the Council, with no indication that a prior request from UN officials was a condition of military action.

56. For general discussion of problems concerning the legitimacy of humanitarian intervention, see R. Lillich (ed.), *Humanitarian Intervention and the United Nations* (London, 1973); Thomas Franck and Nigel Rodley, "After Bangladesh: The Law of Humanitarian Intervention by Military Force," *American Journal of International Law* 67 (1973), p. 275; Michael Akehurst, "Humanitarian Intervention," in Bull (ed.), *Intervention in World Politics,* pp. 95–118; Nigel Rodley (ed.), *To Loose the Bands of Wickedness: International Intervention in Defence of Human Rights* (London, 1992); and Laura Reed and Carl Kaysen (eds.), *Emerging Norms of Justified Intervention* (Cambridge, Mass., 1993).

57. In SC Res. 743 of 21 Feb. 1992, the reference to Charter Article 25, and the fixed (minimum) duration of UNPROFOR's mandate in Croatia, were indications that the Security Council might insist on the continuation of the peacekeeping force, even if the states involved were to withdraw consent. See also SC Res. 761 of 29 June 1992, operative para. 4; and SC Res. 819 of 16 April 1993, operative para. 8.

58. Simon Jones, "General MacKenzie Slams UN's Nine-to-Fivers," *Independent* (London), 31 Jan. 1993.

59. Goulding, "The Evolution of United Nations Peacekeeping," pp. 460, 463; and Paul Lewis, "UN Is Developing Control Centre to Coordinate Growing Peacekeeping Role," *New York Times,* 28 Mar. 1993, p. 10.

60. The UN force in Somalia was the subject of some such charges in 1993. A report from the most critical end of the spectrum is that by a London-based NGO, African Rights, *Somalia: Human Rights Abuses by United Nations Forces* (London, 1993).

61. Boutros-Ghali, statement at New York University, 22 Jan. 1993, p. 3; and speech in Washington, DC, on 25 Mar. 1993. Such an approach was also stressed by Under Secretary–General Goulding, "Evolution of UN Peacekeeping," p. 460. These proposals are more modest than the ambitious suggestions in *Agenda for Peace,* esp. para. 43.

62. See Brian Urquhart, "For a UN Volunteer Military Force," *New York Review of Books,* 10 June 1993, pp. 3–4, and comments in subsequent issues.

63. See, e.g., Commission to Study the Organization of Peace, *Strengthening the United Nations* (New York, 1957).

64. Bill Clinton said while campaigning for the presidency: "Japan and Germany should be made permanent members of the UN Security Council" (address to Foreign Policy Association, 1 Apr. 1992).

65. Statements of numerous countries on the question of Security Council reform are in UN doc. A/48/264 of 20 July 1993, and the many addenda issued in 1993 and 1994. In 1993 the General Assembly established a working group to consider the question.

66. Developed countries are levied at the same rate for peacekeeping as for the regular budget; less-developed countries at 20 percent of their regular rate; least-developed countries at 10 percent. The Permanent Members are assessed the remainder: United States 30.38 percent of peacekeeping costs, France 7.29 percent, UK 6.1 percent, China 0.94 percent. Reallocation of the USSR's 11.44 percent has caused difficulties.

67. A twenty-strong "Chapter VII Consultation Committee" of the General Assembly, to keep an open line between the Security Council and the General Assembly, is proposed by W. Michael Reisman, "The Constitutional Crisis in the United Nations," *American Journal of International Law* 87 (1993), p. 98.

68. *Questions of Interpretation and Application of the 1971 Montreal Convention Arising from the Aerial Incident at Lockerbie (Libya* v. *USA* and *Libya* v. *UK),* Provisional Measures (Orders of 14 Apr. 1992), *ICJ Reports,* 1992, pp. 3 and 114; *Case Concerning Application of the Convention on the Prevention and Punishment of the Crime of Genocide (Bosnia and Herzegovina* v. *Federal Republic of Yugoslavia [Serbia and Montenegro]),* Order Indicating Provisional Measures of Protection, 8 Apr. 1993, and Further Order, 13 Sept. 1993, *ICJ Reports,* 1993.

69. See esp. Adam Watson, *The Evolution of International Society: A Comparative Historical Analysis* (London, 1992).

70. One illustration is L. C. Green, "The Double Standard of the United Nations," *Year Book of World Affairs* 11 (1957), pp. 104–137. The author was principally concerned with indicting the United States and India for embracing double standards in their criticisms of the British role in the 1956 Suez crisis.

71. See, e.g., Anthony Lake, national security adviser to President Clinton, "The Logic of a U.S. Strategy of Enlargement," *International Herald Tribune* (Paris), 24 September 1993, p. 9.

72. Mikhail Gorbachev, "Reality and the Guarantees of a Secure World," *Pravda* (Moscow), 17 Sept. 1987. In this long article the Soviet leader suggested *inter alia* setting up "under the aegis of the UN a mechanism for extensive international verification of compliance with agreements to lessen international tension, limit arms and monitor the military situation in areas of conflict." He also proposed wider use of "UN military observers and UN peacekeeping forces in disengaging the troops of warring sides and monitoring cease-fire and armistice agreements": this proposal did presage an increased use of such forces in subsequent years. See too his speech at the UN General Assembly, 7 Dec. 1988.

73. See, e.g., President Yeltsin's speech at the Security Council summit, 31 Jan. 1992. Facing economic difficulties, and pressure to address conflicts in neighboring states, Russia later became more concerned at the mounting bills for UN peacekeeping and more sceptical generally about UN capacities.

74. On the declaratory tradition, represented par excellence by the UN, as a form of international ethical discourse, see Dorothy V. Jones, "The Declaratory Tradition in Modern International Law," in Terry Nardin and David R. Mapel (eds.), *Traditions of International Ethics* (Cambridge, 1992), pp. 42–61.

75. Contrast, e.g., H. Lauterpacht, *International Law and Human Rights* (London, 1950), with J. S. Watson, "Autointerpretation, Competence, and the Continuing Validity of Article 2(7) of the UN Charter," *American Journal of International Law* 71 (1977), p. 60. See also the Declaration on the Inadmissibility of Intervention in the Domestic Affairs of States and the Protection of their Independence and Sovereignty—GA Res. 2131 (XX) of 21 Dec. 1965.

76. For one such perspective, see Richard A. Falk, Samuel S. Kim, and Saul H. Mendlovitz (eds.), *The United Nations and a Just World Order* (Boulder, Colo., 1991).

77. Note the remarks of Ian Brownlie, "The United Nations as a Form of World Government," *Harvard International Law Journal* 13 (1972), p. 421.

78. On the development of thought and practice about self-determination in the UN framework, see A. Rigo Sureda, *The Evolution of the Right to Self-Determination* (Leiden, 1973); Michla Pomerance, *Self-Determination in Law and Practice: The New Doctrine in the United Nations* (London, 1982); and Karl Doehring, in Bruno Simma et al. (eds.), *Charta der Vereinten Nationen: Kommentar* (Munich, 1991), pp. 20–32.

79. See, e.g., Ethan A. Nadelmann, "Global Prohibition Regimes: The Evolution of Norms in International Society," *International Organization* 44 (1990), pp. 479–526.

80. See generally Aldeeb Abu-Sahlieh et al. (eds.), *Universalité des droits de l'homme et diversité des cultures* (Fribourg, 1984); John Humphrey, *Human Rights and the United Nations: A Great Adventure* (Dobbs Ferry, NY, 1984); Jack

Donnelly, *The Concept of Human Rights* (London, 1985); and R. J. Vincent, *Human Rights and International Relations* (Cambridge, 1986). Sharply different views as to the nature and place of human rights were pressed at the three regional preparatory meetings (particularly the Asian meeting in Bangkok) for the 1993 World Conference on Human Rights held in Vienna. The Vienna Conference itself strongly reaffirmed the universality of human rights, although it did note that "the significance of national and regional particularities and various historical, cultural and religious backgrounds must be borne in mind." A similar balance was struck by the UN General Assembly in Res. 48/141 of 20 Dec. 1993.

81. Boutros-Ghali, *Agenda for Peace*, paras. 9, 81–82. He also discussed this idea in speeches in Boston on 16 Mar. 1993 and Washington, DC, on 25 Mar. 1993.

82. On the link between democracy and peace, see Michael Doyle, "Kant, Liberal Legacies and Foreign Affairs," *Philosophy and Public Affairs* 12 (1983), p. 205.

83. See generally Larry Diamond, Juan Linz, and Seymour Martin Lipset (eds.), *Democracy in Developing Countries*, 4 vols. (Boulder, Colo., 1989–1992).

84. See generally Peterson, *The General Assembly in World Politics*.

85. The affirmation of the principles of international law recognized at Nuremberg is in GA Res. 95 (I) of 11 Dec. 1946. The International Law Commission's formulation of the Nuremberg principles is in *Yearbook of the International Law Commission* (1950), vol. 2, pp. 374–378. The General Assembly's noncommittal response to this formulation is in GA Res. 488 (V) of 12 Dec. 1950. On the subsequent history of this issue, see also *Yearbook of the International Law Commission* (1954), vol. 2, pp. 150–152; and GA Res. 897 (IX) of 4 Dec. 1954. The International Tribunal on Yugoslavia was provided for in SC Res. 827 of 25 May 1993, approving the Statute in UN doc. S/25704 of 3 May 1993.

86. For critical examinations of the idea of "general and complete disarmament," see Hedley Bull, *The Control of the Arms Race* (London, 1961); and John W. Spanier and Joseph L. Nogee, *The Politics of Disarmament* (New York, 1962). See also R. B. Byers and Stanley Ing (eds.), *Arms Limitation and the United Nations* (Toronto, 1982).

87. See esp. Boutros-Ghali, "New Dimensions of Arms Regulation and Disarmament in the Post–Cold War Era: Report of the Secretary-General on the Occasion of Disarmament Week, 27 October 1992," UN doc. A/C.1/47/7, issued by UN Dept. for Public Information, Oct. 1992.

88. See, e.g., the Declaration of 3 Sept. 1991 of the CSCE states; SC Res. 713 of 25 Sept. 1991 and numerous subsequent Security Council resolutions; the Statement on the Situation in Yugoslavia, issued by the North Atlantic Council meeting in Rome, 7–8 Nov. 1991, para. 2; and the Statement of Principles adopted on 26 Aug. 1992 by the London Conference on the Former Socialist Federal Republic of Yugoslavia, para. ii.

89. For a useful political history of UN debates, see Peter Marshall, "The North-South Dialogue: Britain at Odds," in Erik Jensen and Thomas Fisher (eds.), *The United Kingdom—The United Nations* (London, 1990), pp. 159–208.

90. An early study of the importance of the UN's role in conferring legitimacy is Inis Claude, "Collective Legitimization as a Political Function of the United Nations," *International Organization* 20 (1966), p. 367.

91. National liberation movements recognized by the Organization of

African Unity or the League of Arab States were granted observer status in the UN Conference on the Representation of States in Their Relations with International Organizations by the General Assembly "in accordance with the practice of the United Nations"—GA Res. 3247 (XXIX) of 29 Nov. 1974. Numerous other resolutions and administrative decisions also confer status on such groups: the African National Congress (ANC), the PLO, the Pan-Africanist Congress of Azania (PAC), and SWAPO were permitted, for instance, to sign the Final Act of the Third UN Conference on the Law of the Sea in 1982, though not to sign the Convention accompanying it.

92. For materials on these issues respecting the emergence of states from Yugoslavia, see Daniel Bethlehem and Marc Weller (eds.), *The "Yugoslav" Crisis in International Law* (Cambridge, 1994, forthcoming).

93. For an example of useful work on implementation in the human rights field, see Philip Alston (ed.), *The United Nations and Human Rights: A Critical Appraisal* (Oxford, 1992). A long-discussed proposal for the establishment of a UN High Commissioner for Human Rights was finally implemented in GA Res. 48/141 of 20 Dec. 1993, and José Ayala Lasso was appointed to the post in 1994. The International Law Commission has accelerated its work on another long-discussed proposal, the possible establishment of an International Criminal Court.

94. Frank Berman, legal adviser to the UK Foreign and Commonwealth Office, Preface to Hazel Fox and Michael Meyer (eds.), *Effecting Compliance* (London, 1993), p. xii.

95. In *International Law in a Divided World* (Oxford, 1986), Antonio Cassese identifies a traditional "Westphalia model" and a new "UN Charter model" of international law (pp. 396–407) but finds that at present "international law possesses 'two souls', and the second seems incapable of supplanting the first" (p. 4).

96. For a succinct summary of the papal mediation between Argentina and Chile, see *Keesing's Contemporary Archives* (1984), p. 32781; and (1985), p. 33517. See also E. Lauterpacht in *Mélanges Virally* (Paris, 1991), pp. 359–371.

97. Evidence of the vitality of legal development outside the UN framework may be gleaned, for instance, by reference to the fact that the four Geneva Conventions on the protection of victims of war, concluded by states under the auspices of the International Committee of the Red Cross rather than the UN, included 181 parties on 16 June 1993—not counting two ex-Soviet states that are bound through succession but had not yet formally indicated this. The work of The Hague Conference on Private International Law, of the Commonwealth, and of regional intergovernmental organizations may also be cited in this context.

98. *Agenda for Peace*, paras. 60–65.

99. Jan Christian Smuts, *The League of Nations: A Practical Suggestion* (London, 1918), p. 71.

ABOUT THIS OCCASIONAL PAPER

Challenging views that have gained currency since the end of the Cold War, this concise and authoritative study examines the history of the United Nations since 1945, its various roles in international relations, and its approaches to peacekeeping and the use of force.

The authors' distinctive perspective affords an excellent basis for courses and debates on the UN. Judiciously appraising the organization's past performance and future potential—and avoiding the fault of piety, as well as that of UN -bashing—they suggest that the United Nations can be most effective if there is frank recognition of the limits imposed on it by the heterogeneous international society within which it operates.

This monograph completed in February 1994, is an adapted version of the authors' introductory chapter in Roberts and Kingsbury (eds.), *United Nations, Divided World: The UN's Roles in International Relations,* 2d edition (Oxford and New York: Oxford University Press, 1993).

ADAM ROBERTS is Montague Burton Professor of International Relations, University of Oxford, and a fellow of Balliol College. He was previously lecturer in international relations at the London School of Economics and Political Science. His publications include *Nations in Arms: The Theory and Practice of Territorial Defence* and (with Richard Guelff) *Documents on the Laws of War.*

BENEDICT KINGSBURY is professor of law at the Duke University School of Law. He was previously lecturer in law at Oxford University and a fellow of Exeter College. A specialist in international law and human rights, he is completing a book on indigenous peoples in international law. His publications include *The International Politics of the Environment* (edited with Andrew Hurrell) and *Hugo Grotius and International Relations* (edited with Hedley Bull and Adam Roberts).

THE INTERNATIONAL PEACE ACADEMY

The International Peace Academy is an independent, nonpartisan, international institution devoted to the promotion of peaceful and multilateral approaches to the resolution of international as well as internal conflicts. IPA plays a facilitating role in efforts to settle conflicts, providing a middle ground where the options for settling particular conflicts are explored and promoted in an informal setting. Other activities of the organization include public forums; training seminars on conflict resolution and peacekeeping; and research and workshops on collective security, regional and internal conflicts, peacemaking, peacekeeping, and nonmilitary aspects of security.

In fulfilling its mission, IPA works closely with the United Nations, regional and other international organizations, governments, and parties to conflicts. The work of IPA is further enhanced by its ability to draw on a worldwide network of eminent persons comprising government leaders, statesmen, business leaders, diplomats, military officers, and scholars. In the aftermath of the Cold War, there is a general awakening to the enormous potential of peaceful and multilateral approaches to resolving conflicts. This has given renewed impetus to the role of IPA.

IPA is governed by an international board of directors. Financial support for the work of the organization is provided primarily by philanthropic foundations, as well as individual donors.

INTERNATIONAL PEACE ACADEMY

OCCASIONAL PAPER SERIES

Available from the International Peace Academy, 777 United Nations Plaza, New York, New York 10017 (212-949-8480):

The Future of Peacekeeping, Indar Jit Rikhye
Paths to Peace in Afghanistan: The Geneva Accords and After, Selig S. Harrison
The Financing of United Nations Peacekeeping Operations: The Need for a Sound Financial Basis, Susan R. Mills
United Nations Peacekeeping: Management and Operations, F. T. Liu
Negotiations Before Peacekeeping, Cameron R. Hume

Available from Lynne Rienner Publishers, 1800 30th Street, Boulder, Colorado 80301 (303-444-6684):

The United Nations in a Turbulent World, James N. Rousenau
United Nations Peacekeeping and the Non-Use of Force, F. T. Liu
The Wave of the Future: The United Nations and Naval Peacekeeping, Robert Stephens Staley II
Political Order in Post-Communist Afghanistan, William Maley and Fazel Haq Saikal
Seeking Peace from Chaos: Humanitarian Intervention in Somalia, Samuel M. Makinda
Aftermath of the Gulf War: An Assessment of UN Action, Ian Johnstone